PROPHETS AND RULERS

being

BOOK TWO

of

BACKGROUND TO THE BIBLE

Based on the contents and requirements of the major Agreed Syllabuses

by

Bernard R. Youngman

(*author*, "*Teaching Religious Knowledge*")

HULTON EDUCATIONAL PUBLICATIONS

TO THOSE WHO READ THIS BOOK

THE recorded story of the Bible falls naturally into four parts: from Abraham to Solomon, from the Divided Kingdom to the Coming of Christ, the Life and Teaching of Christ, and the Spread of Christianity.

The books in this series follow this sequence:
Book   I: Patriarchs, Judges and Kings.
Book II: Prophets and Rulers.
Book III: The Palestine of Jesus.
Book IV: Spreading the Gospel.

What this book and the others in this series set out to do is to provide background information of all kinds about the Land and the People of the Bible, their lives, occupations, homes, customs, beliefs, and so on.   Lots of pictures—photographs and drawings—have been included to help you to " see " more vividly the events and experiences of these Bible people, in the hope that you will realise more clearly just what God meant to them in their days and what He might mean to you and to me today.

Be sure to study the Bible passages given you in each chapter—that is something you must not fail to do.

ACKNOWLEDGMENTS

Grateful acknowledgments are made to the following for the use of copyright photographs:
Radio Times Hulton Picture Library, Ewing Galloway, Paul Popper, Alan Cash, Mirrorpic, Black Star, Donald McLeish, Pictorial Press, J. C. Rogerson, E.N.A., The British Museum, The Hague Museum, Shell Photographic Unit.

The drawings were prepared by Y. M. Poulton, P. Savoie and T. A. Steele, to whom thanks are also due.

©

Bernard R. Youngman

First published 1956
Reprinted 1957
Reprinted 1958
Reprinted 1959
Reprinted 1960
Reprinted 1961
Reprinted 1963
Reprinted 1965
Reprinted 1967
Reprinted 1971
Reprinted 1976
Reprinted 1978

ISBN 0 7175 0416 6 (Limp)
ISBN 0 7175 0417 4 (Board)

HULTON EDUCATIONAL PUBLICATIONS, LTD. Raans Road, Amersham, Bucks
Made and printed in Great Britain by William Clowes and Sons Limited, London, Beccles and Colchester

CONTENTS

INTRODUCTION

THIS book is called *Prophets and Rulers*, and covers the period of Jewish history between the Divided Kingdom and the Coming of Christ.

In Book I we saw how the Jews gradually learned that Yahweh was more powerful than their other gods; but perhaps the most they grasped was that He was at least as good as the best of themselves. It was the prophets who led them into a closer understanding of Him; some of the rulers also had a good deal to say and do in this matter. The people felt that Yahweh, having brought them out of Egypt, had made them a chosen people, so nothing harmful could happen to them; they did not see that other nations might have felt like that about their gods, nor did they appear to give all their chief worship to Yahweh Who had been so good to them. Having settled in Palestine, the Jews, learning from the Canaanites the ways of agriculture, had accepted also the Canaanite gods of fertility, in the belief that this would enable them to obtain good crops; these they worshipped alongside Yahweh at their "high places" and shrines in the open countryside. It was a common custom for tribes —and even nations—to take over any god of another people that might be expected to show special favour or power.

In this next period of the great prophets the people were to learn that Yahweh was not like these other gods; He did not need sacrifices, special gifts and payment. He only wanted trust and faith and goodness (see Is. i, 11–17; Mic. vi, 6–8). Up to this time, as we saw in Book I, the kings—Saul, David and Solomon—had followed in the steps of the patriarchs and judges as spiritual leaders of the people. To a large extent they had failed, for the Jews were still quick to accept false gods and slow to believe entirely in Yahweh as the one true God. The duty of bringing them back to Him was now in the hands of the prophets.

Some people would say that a prophet was a fore-teller; it would be truer to say that he was a *forth*-teller. He saw events as they were and told the truth about them. Although often humble and uneducated, he spoke for God with a strange understanding of events that urged him to proclaim what would certainly happen to the people if they did not give up their wrong ways of living and return to Yahweh. As God's spokesman he denounced their wickedness as being the opposite of what He wanted; it did not matter how correct they were in their forms of worship, how elaborate were their rituals and gifts; what was needed was kindness and justice to all men and absolute obedience to Him. God's spiritual laws could not be ignored or broken, and, if necessary, to teach them this lesson Yahweh would go so far as to allow the destruction of the whole nation— although He would save a handful of loyal servants to begin the rebuilding of a new Israel. In other words, if Israel would not listen, she was doomed.

Some advisers and leaders of the nation have already been met in Book I. There were Aaron and Miriam and the unknown prophet in the story of Gideon; Samuel and Nathan in the story of David. There were also groups of "ecstatic prophets", so called because of their habit of working themselves into a frenzy; Saul joined a band of these prophets. But we do not meet any really great prophets until the middle of the ninth century B.C., when the events of the time brought forth these fearless speakers who made great efforts to bring the people "back to their senses".

Some of these great men had followers, professional prophets or guilds, who lived in groups. Elisha joined one of these bands. Some of them retained and wrote down the fiery words and warnings of their leaders, and through them and the scribes we have had preserved for us their very words uttered in denunciation, encouragement and advice—and how powerful and moving these words sound in our ears today. Through them we see God and His people in times of great dangers and tragic events. The prophets knew God as individual, obedient servants; their duty was to bring the nation into obedience too; but how hard a task that was we shall now see.

CHAPTER 1

THE DIVIDED KINGDOM

(1 Kings xii, 1–20, 25–33; xiv, 25–31; xvi, 15–33; xxi; 2 Kings ix, 16–37)

WHEN Solomon died c. 930 B.C. his son Rehoboam went to Shechem to be anointed king. There he found waiting to talk with him Jeroboam, who had fled to Egypt after the failure of his rebellion against Solomon (Book I) and had now returned from exile in order to lead the people against the new king. The people certainly had much of which to complain—taxes, forced labour, injustices of all kinds: Jeroboam now asked that Rehoboam should be less of a tyrant than his father and ease the people's burdens.

Rehoboam missed the opportunity of winning the support of the people, for after three days—having taken the worst possible advice from the young men—he threatened to rule even more harshly than his father had done; he would drive the people with whips tipped with spikes that scourged them as painfully and cruelly as the stings of scorpions. The people shouted their defiance and rebellion and stoned to death Adoram, the hated officer in charge of forced labour.

"A Lamp in Israel"

Rehoboam fled to Jerusalem; the city was in the territory of Benjamin, which now united with Judah and remained loyal to the throne. This loyalty was fortunate for the king. There had been a prophecy which said that these tribes would remain true followers of the "line of David", and that David would have "a lamp always before Me" This strange reference reminds us of the great fear of darkness these people always had. In the desert they had been grateful for the "pillar of fire by night" to drive away evil spirits; if there were no light in a house it was a sign of emptiness, death and destruction. When Jeremiah speaks of threatened devastation from Babylon he uses the same idea—"I will cause to perish from them ... the light of the lamp." David had been promised a lamp in

Jerusalem; the prophecy was fulfilled when Rehoboam established himself in the city (see also 2 Kings viii, 19; 1 Kings xv, 4; Prov. xiii, 9).

The Two Kingdoms

The land was now split in two; it remained so until its final destruction. The two tribes forming the Southern Kingdom of Judah remained loyal to Rehoboam; the other ten tribes forming the Northern Kingdom of Israel (sometimes called Ephraim) went over to Jeroboam. This division was to some extent due to the fact that Palestine had never been a complete whole. The Jebusites and Canaanites and other tribes had from the first separated the Hebrews (as they were then called) from one another, so there was no national unity; there had been rivalry between the two parts even in David's time (see 2 Sam. xix, 40–43). The formation of the country, with its hills and valleys and the Jordan rift, had also prevented real geographical union. There was jealousy, too, for Judah had never been called upon to pay taxes and do forced labour in the quarries, and the northerners had been angry at the king's

A prophet as he might have appeared to the people of Israel and Judah in the eighth century.

7

These are figurines or teraphim—little models of false gods, worn or used to bring their owners "good luck". The Bible calls them baalim or ashtoreth. These two probably represent Astarte, the goddess of fertility. (1 Kings xi, 5; Isa. xliv, 10.)

favouritism. Above all, the two kingdoms had different interests and occupations. Judah had difficulty in obtaining food, and made the best of her poor soil in agriculture—farming, sheep-rearing, vineyards and olive orchards; her communities were for the most part small, in villages and walled cities. Israel, to the north, was more aware of her neighbours—Phoenicia, Syria, Assyria—and trade with these countries flourished; wealth came from taxes paid by the caravans that had to pass through the main routes of the kingdom, and there was normal trading in large cities like Samaria, Bethel and Damascus.

Bull-worship

To make sure of full control of his new possessions, Jeroboam would not let the people go up to Jerusalem to worship at their feasts; he set up for them two metal bulls—"golden calves". Bull-worship was familiar in Egypt and Syria as the symbol of nature-worship and the Canaanites used it too; for the Israelites to worship golden calves representing Yahweh was a dangerous link with heathen worship, and with his bull-idols at Dan and Bethel Jeroboam encouraged the people to drift away from the true worship of Yahweh. Even his priests were no longer Levites, whereas it had been laid down by the Law of Moses that

members of the tribe of Levi were the only people who could be priests of Yahweh; this breaking of the Law made the rift even wider. Jeroboam betrayed his people with the very words Aaron had used when the Hebrews had worshipped the golden calf in Sinai—"Behold thy gods, O Israel, which brought thee out of the land of Egypt." Division of the kingdom was now complete—Israel in the north and Judah in the south.

It is not surprising that the Northern Kingdom went over to the worship of false gods and idols (see 1 Kings xv, 34; xvi, 26). But so did the Southern Kingdom (1 Kings xiv, 23). Nor are we surprised to learn that the two kingdoms warred with each other and caused great hardship and bitterness throughout the whole land. Shishak of Egypt who had befriended Jeroboam invaded Judah. He forced Rehoboam to pay tribute and took away golden and silver vessels from the Temple itself, even though the king had his body-guard to help him. Some scholars think he may have destroyed the Ark, for it is not mentioned again in these accounts. Shishak recorded his victories and also his invasion of Megiddo and Lachish—which Rehoboam had evidently fortified—on the walls of the temple of Amon

A whip of scorpions. The pieces of metal in each thong were meant to cut into the flesh. Nine hundred years after Rehoboam, Christ was scourged with whips like this.

A lamp with seven pinchings for seven wicks. One of the simplest kind, it dates from the period of the Divided Kingdom.

A vase shaped like a bull idol. This gives us some idea of the golden bull idols set up by Jeroboam in Dan and Bethel.

(Amen-Ra) at Karnak. We shall hear more of these places later.

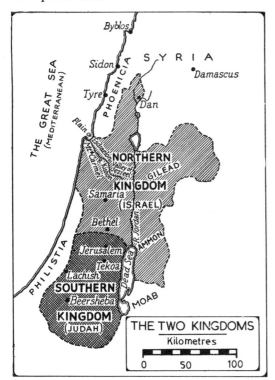

The Divided Kingdom. Notice how near to the Northern Kingdom are Syria and Phoenicia and how Judah (the Southern Kingdom) lies to the east of the main coast highways.

Samaria, the Capital

Jeroboam fared badly also. Invasion from the Syrians brought treachery and bloodshed. When he died there was much fighting for control of the kingdom and kings followed one another in quick succession. Then Omri, seizing the throne in 880 B.C., became king. By trade and war he brought great power to the Northern Kingdom. He built as his capital city Samaria—a "city on a hill". It overlooked the Plain of Sharon; we are told that the entrance to the city was a single gate let in the walls on the steepest side of the hill and protected by a special tower. The walls of the city were three metres thick. The only means of conquering it was by starving out the defenders; it was well named "watch-tower". Even the Assyrians called the Northern Kingdom "Omriland". The building of Samaria is the only thing about Omri that is mentioned in the Bible; the city has been excavated and in the palace beautiful ivory furnishings have been found, both solid and inlaid. But Omri must have had great success in his other undertakings, for the famous Moabite Stone (found in A.D. 1868) gives a long list of lands conquered and held by him; the Stone tells of the conquests of the King of Moab, serving his god Chemosh (this was Ruth's god, you will remember). Part of the inscription on it reads: "And Chemosh said unto me, Go, take Nebo against Israel. . . . And I fought against it . . . and I took the vessels of

**A "city on a hill".
Samaria was situated
like this (p. 9).**

Yahweh. . . ." In 876 B.C. Ashur-nasir-pal—perhaps the most cruel of the kings of Assyria—
marched through the Fertile Crescent and took
tribute from Phoenicia; so Omri formed alliances
between neighbouring kingdoms to prevent
Assyria from becoming too dangerous. His son
Ahab followed his example and eventually
united Phoenicia, Syria, Israel and Judah—but
much was to happen before this.

Meanwhile Samaria was growing in importance
as a fine trading city, and Ahab inherited considerable wealth and power when he became the
new King of Israel.

EXPRESSION WORK

1. Read Jer. vii, Amos, iii, 11; v, 14; viii, 11,
   Isa. ii, 6 ff., Mic. ii, Hos. vi; list from these
   what the prophets themselves say is their
   work.
2. What kinds of prophets are mentioned in the
   Bible? What was the special work of each
   type?
3. Act the scene between Jeroboam and Rehoboam.
4. Submit the question Rehoboam has to
   answer to the two groups of counsellors in
   turn; let these then discuss it and advise the
   king.
5. Find from reference books all you can about
   lamps in the Bible.
6. Draw a map of the Divided Kingdom; shade
   the two parts clearly.
7. Model or draw priests offering sacrifices to
   the bull-idol.
8. In what ways were Syria and Israel "buffer
   states"? How was it that Judah escaped this
   particular position?

9. Letter and learn any prophecy or striking
   phrases spoken by one of these early
   prophets.
10. What do these words mean: "And Chemosh
    said unto me, Go, take Nebo against
    Israel . . ."?
11. Discuss Jeroboam's action in setting up bull-
    gods.

    or

    Write to a friend in Jerusalem explaining
    why you will not be seeing him at the next
    Feast.
12. Find all you can about Megiddo and Karnak.
    Write notes and illustrate with pictures and
    drawings where possible.

**Ashur-nasir-pal II, King of
the Assyrians in the ninth
century B.C. Omri made an
alliance against this very
cruel king.**

CHAPTER 2

ELIJAH

(1 Kings xi, 26–40; xii; xvi, 23–33; xvii; xviii, 1–46; xix, 1–18; xxi, 1–19; xxii)

AHAB had married Jezebel in order to ally Israel with Phoenicia (see map). Jezebel was the daughter of the priest-king and a worshipper of Baal; baal means lord or spirit-owner. It was believed by many of the people of those days that a spirit lived in a spring or by a well, and "owned" it; this meant that the spirit had to be worshipped to make sure that it was helpful and good to the people who lived near the spring or well and needed to use its water.

A Wicked Queen

Domineering and cruel, Jezebel brought with her her Phoenician Baal-Melkart, a sun- and sea-god; his image was placed in the Temple in Samaria itself; Ashtart (Astarte) was already being worshipped as the goddess of fertility alongside the bull-idol representing Yahweh. But Jezebel was not content to have her god worshipped as one of two or three; Melkart was to be the chief god, and worship of Yahweh was to be stamped out altogether. She even brought her own Baal prophets—four hundred and fifty of them—introduced child-sacrifice once more, and murdered and persecuted the prophets and followers of Yahweh, who fled and hid in the caves outside the city; these men were secretly looked after by Obadiah. Jezebel wanted baal-worship to be the national religion and was prepared to go to any lengths to make it so. Jeroboam "had made Israel to sin", but she was on the point of blotting out completely the spiritual life of the Northern Kingdom. Ahab, a brave soldier but a weak king, let her do exactly as she pleased.

It was just as she seemed to be succeeding that she was suddenly and dramatically challenged by one of the greatest men in the Bible—Elijah.

Elijah comes into the Bible narrative quite unexpectedly. He was a Tishbite (or Jabeshite) from the desert highlands of Gilead, across the Jordan (1 Kings i, 8). His name means "My God—

A Phoenician war-galley, carved on a bas-relief at the time of Sennacherib. The Phoenicians were expert sailors and traders.

Jezebel brought her false Phoenician gods to the Northern Kingdom. This is a terra-cotta model of her favourite—Melkart.

Israel, by his dress and perhaps by his dialect, for she spoke to him in the name of Yahweh—"As Yahweh, thy God, liveth . . . " She did as Elijah told her, despite her first doubts, and shared her food—meal and oil. The meal was barley meal, in a pot—not a barrel as we know it. The cruse was a small earthenware jar, the oil—olive oil. The raising to life of the child is a gentle, moving and happy incident in the life of this fierce, stern prophet.

The famine had come, despite the wailing prayers of the priests of Melkart to their god who was the "spirit-owner" of the rain. With the drought had come anxiety and fear; nearly three years had gone by and there was starvation and desperation. The ground was brick-hard, the waterless wadis were cracked deeper than they had ever been, and the hill-slopes were brown with scorched vegetation; cattle and sheep and people died. . . .

Mt. Carmel

Ahab put the blame on Elijah; but Elijah was to prove to him that he himself was very much to blame for allowing Jezebel to do so much wrong. The prophet made his challenge to the king. Mt. Carmel was well chosen; it was a sacred mountain, overlooking the sea to the north and the Plain of Esdraelon to the east. Its hill-slopes would normally have been covered with growing crops, and sheep and cattle would have been grazing on its soft grass. But on a small plateau near the top (the spot is still to be seen, 490 metres up the mountain, and is called "the

Yahweh". It was evident that Elijah was not going to stand by and see his people forsake Yahweh; nor would he hide in the caves with Obadiah's prophets. He knew that without Yahweh Israel could not exist as a nation, and he was determined to save her.

Elijah and the Widow

Elijah was sure that the threatened famine was a sign of Yahweh's displeasure, and the prophet foretold drought and distress unless and until the people turned to Him. He then moved to a quiet spot by Brook Cherith and was able to live on the food dropped by the ravens on their flight there. He decided to go to Phoenicia, the land of Baal-Melkart. So we follow this gaunt, sunburnt man; as a man of God, a prophet of Yahweh, he wore his hair long and flowing beneath his headdress, and over his shoulders was slipped the simple sheepskin or goatskin cloak (his mantle) which, later, he was to hand to Elisha, his faithful follower. He crossed the Jordan, having moved along its eastern bank, and travelled westwards to the coast near Sidon. At a little village, Zarephath, he paused; a woman came near him and he asked for water—a common request in the east when travellers were hot and thirsty. She was gathering sticks—possibly pieces of acacia bush —"at the gate", just outside the village. She must have recognised Elijah as coming from

An example of Israelite pottery of this period. It was always much better formed and finished than was the pottery of Judah. Why?

The western foothills of Mount Carmel, overlooking the Great Sea (Mediterranean). Even in the days of Elijah there was probably a lighthouse. Why? What are the plants in the foreground?

place of burning") Elijah faced the people, crowded among the rocks, weary, frightened, staring at the parched ground and wilting under the hot sun. Nearby the prophets of Baal waited, unaware of the disastrous defeat that was to be theirs by the end of the day; already they were fingering their knives and calling on each other in fierce excitement. The altar to Yahweh had been destroyed and one to Melkart put in its place.

The Great Challenge

The Bible describes the scene that followed in wonderful language. Elijah heightens the drama. Water was precious enough at any time, but just now it was beyond price. Yet he told the people to pour it into the ditch and on the altar—on the twelve stones he had reared to represent the twelve tribes. The impending storm was heralded by fierce streaks of lightning—always in the Bible called "the fire of the Lord". The fire of the Lord and the prayer of Elijah did what the Baal-

Melkart and his screaming prophets could not do. Then came the dramatic challenge to the people. Read it aloud, in 1 Kings xviii, and feel the exciting climax. How long were they "to halt and totter, first on one knee and then on the other"? (This probably referred to the steps in some of the heathen dances around the altars of the false gods, and even more closely to the very dances of the frenzied baal-prophets.) The people must make a decision for or against Yahweh. And they shouted, "Yahweh, He is God! Yahweh, He is God!"

Elijah's calm confidence in Yahweh stood out boldly against the foolish frenzy of the prophets of Baal. The storm had ended the drought. The Kishon overflowed its banks, as it had done many years before when Sisera's army threatening Deborah and Barak had been caught and drowned; Ahab's chariot was almost swamped as it ploughed through the boggy marshland, heading for Jezreel, his summer capital. Elijah, in the excitement of victory, ran in front of the chariot for the whole 27 kilometres. Wells and streams and wadis filled up—the rain had come! Yahweh, He was God!

The "Still, Small Voice"

Jezebel was furious. Realising his immediate danger, Elijah fled—through Beersheba and on to Horeb, the place of Moses. This was where the Covenant between the people and Yahweh had been made—and where, for Elijah, it might now end. We are not certain if Horeb was indeed Sinai, or whether it was perhaps Mt. Hor, south of the Dead Sea. By now, Elijah was dejected; he wanted to die. He had forgotten the prophets in hiding awaiting a leader. He was asking where was Yahweh, after all? Not in the hurricane, or in the earthquake, or in the lightning; God was in the "still small voice" speaking to Elijah in that strange inner way that we sometimes call "conscience". The real translation of this familiar phrase is "a sound of gentle stillness"—which makes it very clear that God comes to us in moments of quiet. Elijah was learning that Yahweh was not just another god; He had a purpose and claimed obedience from His people. And Elijah was to see to it that this was made clear to them also. He heard, too, the judgments of Yahweh upon Ahab and the nation: then he returned to Israel to continue his work for Yahweh.

Naboth

The story of Naboth's vineyard is another familiar incident in the life and work of Elijah. Ahab's summer palace at Jezreel overlooked the vineyard; the king must many times have seen Naboth mounting his watch-tower, looking out for marauders or signs of rain and generally supervising his property. The vineyard must have been in Naboth's family for years, since the Israelites had come to Palestine. It was an inheritance that he could never give up except to a kinsman (Num. xxxvi, 1–8; Lev. xxv, 27, 28). But Ahab wanted the vineyard; it was so handy alongside his own garden, and he had only to make a new gate into it. Yet, though he was king, he recognised Naboth's right to refuse; he made a fair offer for exchange, but Naboth held out; so Ahab sulked on his ivory-backed divan and behaved like a spoilt child.

Jezebel's Plot

Jezebel found him in this mood. Ahab told her what had happened; he had wanted the vineyard

Here is a fellah (peasant) attending to his grapes. The plants spread over the ground and the bunches are lifted on forked sticks to clear the dust. Note the wall.

The kind of watch-tower from which Naboth gazed at his vineyard.

sent letters to the chief men of the city, written on skins and bearing the king's seal; two lying witnesses were to bring false evidence against Naboth. As a result, Naboth was accused of treason and murdered. Savage pariah dogs licked the blood of Naboth as he lay stoned to death outside the city. So Ahab obtained his vineyard, but he lost his peace of mind. In sackcloth and ashes, the signs of great grief, he heard the dreadful prophecies from the lips of the stern prophet who stood alone in the power of Yahweh against the king himself.

Elijah Chooses Elisha

Elijah had to find a successor; he could not carry out all the work necessary to restore the nation to Yahweh. He probably already knew Elisha and found him handling a plough as one of a team of twelve (1 Kings xix, 19 ff.). He threw his mantle of goatskin or sheepskin over Elisha's shoulders to show that he was choosing the young man as a disciple and follower. A father frequently passed on to his son his simlah, his striped outer jacket, and Elijah was making it clear that Elisha was to take over his work. Elisha then burned the plough, yoke and goad— "the instruments of oxen"—to make a fire on which he roasted the oxen. As a mere servant he

for a herb garden where he could grow lettuce and chicory, watercress, even onions and garlic, and—so that Jezebel might be sure of having spices for seasoning her food—cinnamon, dill and mint. But he could not have it. Jezebel saw Ahab's sense of justice as nothing but weakness. She determined that the king should have the vineyard and made a wicked plot to get it. She

Ahab sulked on his couch. Later, Amos accused the wealthy of "sprawling on ivory divans", drinking wine and listening to music, but ignoring the needs of the poor.

A Hebrew seal (1 Kings xxi, 8). This is a sacred beetle-shaped one, called a scaraboid, sometimes used as ornaments or beads. Probably brought from Egypt to Palestine during the time of the Hyksos kings (Book I, p. 29).

"poured water on the hands of Elijah"—a common duty in those days. Although evidently a rich young farmer, he was now prepared to follow his new master and to learn what was needed of him in the service of Yahweh.

EXPRESSION WORK

1. Write and act the scene in which Jezebel puts her plans before the priests of Baal.
2. "Ahab had the makings of a fine king, but his wife ruined him." Discuss this.
3. Draw Elijah meeting the woman at Zarephath.
   or
   Draw the scene on Mt. Carmel.
4. Write a Radio Script on "The Challenge of Elijah".
5. Pretend you are Elijah at Horeb. Speak your thoughts aloud.
   or
   Find the hymn "Dear Lord and Father of mankind". Write out and learn the verse that seems to refer to Elijah's experience on Mt. Horeb.
   or

Find in the oratorio *Elijah* the aria (song) that tells of Elijah's despair; play a gramophone recording of this if you can obtain it.
6. Prepare the Mt. Carmel scene for Dramatic Reading. You will need a Narrator and individual characters and groups to represent the priests of Baal and the people. Arrange to give the reading in a Morning Assembly.
7. Describe the choosing of Elisha as a close friend of the young prophet might have told it to other members of the ploughing team.
8. Draw Elisha ploughing.
9. Prepare and act in modern language the discussion between Ahab and Naboth.
10. Draw or model Naboth looking from his watch-tower.
11. Write Jezebel's message; seal it with Ahab's seal.
12. Pretend you are the men paid to accuse Naboth. Prepare your plan of action. Meet again and talk about his death with some misgivings.

Returning from the day's work. Look closely at the simple plough carried across the back of the tireless donkey.

Here is an impression such as Jezebel made with Ahab's seal. It says "(belonging) to Shemac, Servant of Jeroboam", King of Israel, 786 – 745 B.C.

CHAPTER 3

ELISHA

(2 Kings ii, 1–15; iv, 8–37; v, 1–16; vi, 8–23; xiii, 14–20)

ELISHA'S special work was to carry out the other two orders of Yahweh—to anoint Jehu, a ruthless soldier who would rebel against Ahab and root out the false Phoenician worship of Melkart; and to go to Damascus to meet a Syrian captain, Hazael, who would be the future ruler of Syria when he, too, had rebelled against his king.

Elijah's Last Journey

The prophet journeyed with Elijah from Gilgal to Bethel. At Bethel they met a group of young men training to be prophets who warned Elisha that he would soon lose his beloved master. Elisha felt that this was true and insisted upon staying with Elijah, through the Jordan valley to Jericho, where they met yet another group who gave him the same warning. They came to the Jordan at the "place of baptism"—a ford over the river; this was possibly the ford across which Joshua had passed many years before, when the Hebrews began to enter Palestine. Across the river loomed Mt. Nebo where centuries before Moses had left his people.

Here it was that the two prophets now paused, and in answer to Elijah's question, Elisha asked for "a double portion" of the older man's spirit. He did not want to be twice as great as Elijah; he was merely asking for the share of the first-born, which was twice that of the rest of the sons; for Elisha was to succeed Elijah as a son did his father and as the man responsible to Yahweh (Deut. xxi, 17).

Elisha's test of worthiness was to see the chariot and horses of fire in what may have been a furious storm of lightning. His exclamation "the chariot of Israel; the horsemen thereof" appears to be a proverb or saying; Elisha meant that Elijah was of greater worth to the nation than all its horses and chariots. And to him, too, it meant that the horses and chariots of the Lord of Hosts were the true defence of Israel (1 Kings xiii, 14).

Thus Elijah passed from the great events of this time. But the Jews have always remembered him. We recall that he was one of those at the Transfiguration of Christ (Matt. xvi, 14; Luke i, 27; ix, 8, 19; John i, 21). Even today, at every

The Jordan at a point where it would be easy to ford. At a similar spot Elisha said goodbye to Elijah.

17

The Shunammite woman provided a room for Elisha on the house-top; it was reached by outside steps. Note the parapet (Deut. xxii, 8).

Passover Feast, a chair is placed for Elijah and every so often someone goes to the door to see if he is waiting to come in.

Elisha Begins His Work

When Elisha—whose name means "God is Salvation"—finally put on his master's mantle he showed his willingness to continue Elijah's work; the "schools of prophets" or prophet guilds also accepted him as one of themselves having special authority as a leader, and frequently he sat with them "round the great pot" at Gilgal (2 Kings iv, 38–41).

Elisha, bald (2 Kings ii, 23) and weather-tanned, was a friendly man. Unlike Elijah, he had grown up amongst the people; he was the son of a rich farmer and knew what it was to move amongst his neighbours. He visited the walled cities (2 Kings vi, 13–19, 32), and even had his own house in Samaria. He "went about doing good", and the stories about him are for the most part warm, kind and human. One cannot imagine Elijah having any interest in music, but Elisha seems to have enjoyed it (2 Kings iii, 15).

The Shunammite Woman

The story of the Shunammite woman reveals much about the prophet. You will find it in 2 Kings iv, 8–37. Shunem lies in the north of the Valley of Jezreel, high in the hills and facing south, twenty-four kilometres from Carmel. The woman was the wife of a wealthy farmer whose fields lay terraced on the hill-slopes; she herself had connections with rich people too. The "little room" made for Elisha was reached by an outside stairway of stone steps; it contained a thin mattress or pallet that could be rolled up by day,

This is how the Shunammite woman often took her small son on journeys. As she was very rich she had a white ass.

a table, a stool and the all-important olive-oil shoe-shaped or seven-pinched lamp—for even Elisha would not sleep in the dark if he could avoid it. Gehazi was Elisha's servant and disciple; we do not form a very high opinion of Gehazi. The woman's son, whose birth Elisha had foretold, caught sunstroke in the fierce hot noonday sun. His father was in the harvest field reaping and threshing corn. He was watching the heavy threshing instrument, a board studded with flints and pieces of iron, dragged by oxen over the reaped corn (see Isa. xli, 15). He wondered why his wife should want to go to Elisha; it was not a feast-day or a new moon, not even a Sabbath. She rode on an ass, probably a white one, as wealthy people always did, her servant urging it along with his right hand on its flank and in his left a stick or goad to encourage speed. The journey was thirty-two kilometres and her anxiety on arrival made Elisha act quickly.

He told Gehazi to "tighten up his belt"—that is, to tuck into his girdle the folds of his cloak so that he could hurry. He was not to stop to speak to anyone. This seems discourteous, but what Elisha really meant was, "Be as quick as you can." Greetings and salutations in Palestine, even today, are most elaborate; there are certain routine phrases and actions that must be observed (see Book I, p. 12), and to cut these short would certainly be rude; the only way to avoid them would be to hurry along with eyes to the ground. Jesus had much the same idea in mind when He told His disciples to "salute no man by the way" (Luke x, 4).

In 2 Kings iv, 29–31 we read that Gehazi failed to revive the child with Elisha's staff, despite the fact that he may have believed it was the sign of authority; it is evident that he had no real faith in Elisha—perhaps not in Yahweh either. Elisha had faith and we are glad that he brought happiness to the Shunammite woman who had been so kind to him.

The Slave-maid

The story of Naaman is set against an historical background (2 Kings v). The Syrians (see map) were frequently at war with Israel and whenever possible in their forays had dragged off men, women and children to be their slave-workers. That is how the little girl in this story came to be a waiting-maid to the wife of Naaman, a captain in the Syrian army. Naaman was a leper. Leprosy was a dread disease of the skin for which in those days there was no known cure; it was infectious and painful. Soon Naaman would have to leave his wife, home and companions, and live alone in some wild corner of the hills—an outcast.

The serving-maid remembered Elisha in Samaria and Yahweh, her own God. She must have been fond of her master and mistress, who had evidently treated her kindly from the first. Perhaps Naaman agreed to go to the man of God as a last hope. The King of Syria sent by Naaman a letter of introduction—probably written on a

Elisha's Fountain. Read 2 Kings ii, 19–22.

This is a N. Syrian god or baal, made of bronze and dating from the time of the Exodus (see Book I, Ch. 9).

when they were taken to Babylon. So if Naaman wanted to worship Yahweh, as he now said he would, he must rear an altar to Him on the soil of Israel. He would have to continue at least lip-service to Rimmon, the thunder-god, whom he had worshipped all his life. It is possible that he set up his new altar on the earth he took with him, at the temple in Damascus and alongside the altar to his Syrian god. Perhaps you wonder, as many people do, what happened to the little serving-maid; no one knows, although it seems difficult to believe that she was not rewarded in some very wonderful way.

The story of Naaman ends with the dreadful punishment of Gehazi, which some people think gives a wrong impression of God. Probably Gehazi became a leper through contact with Naaman or through handling some of the gifts he took from the captain, but his cunning was given as the reason. The old writers often looked for some kind of sin or wrong action to account for a misfortune, and the scribes probably felt that Gehazi had deserved his leprosy. We shall see how the friends of Job told him his sorrows had come because of some secret sin in his life.

skin and sealed with the royal seal—to the King of Israel, who was perhaps startled to see the captain in his war chariot. He was suspicious of the letter, for he missed the point of what the little girl had said. "Behold Naaman . . .", said the letter, "that *thou* mayest recover him of his leprosy." But it was not the king who could do it; it was the prophet. Elisha reassured the king and gave Naaman instructions that he did not like. He refused to dip himself in Jordan. There were at least two other rivers, the Abana and the Pharpar, flowing eastwards from Damascus, both clear and clean—why could he not bathe in one of those? But in answer to the pleadings of his servants, who were anxious to see their beloved master healed, Naaman went down to the muddy waters of Jordan, entered them and came out with his skin like "that of a little child".

Naaman Turns to Yahweh

The captain's request for two mules' burdens of Israel's earth seems strange until we remember that in those days it was a common belief that a god of any country could be worshipped only on the soil of that country. Even the Jews in Exile believed at first that Yahweh had forsaken them

Jezebel was thrown from a lattice window not unlike this one on a modern building.

A scavenging Syrian dog; the kind that licked the blood of Ahab and Jezebel.

But Jesus has something to say about this idea, as you will find in John ix, 1 and Luke xiii, 1–5.

Outwitting the Enemy!

A third familiar and popular story of Elisha is that in which he outwits the Syrians at Dothan (2 Kings iii, 9–20). Dothan was sixteen kilometres north of Samaria, in a valley followed by the great caravan routes connecting Egypt and Assyria through Damascus. We have heard of this town before, in the story of Joseph (Book I). Benhadad, King of Syria, often found that his invasion plans made "in thy bedchamber"—that is, in secret—were known to the powerful King of Israel, and eventually decided that the "culprit" was Elisha, who must be captured without delay. He sent an *army* to Dothan— for one man! They surrounded the city by night, planning to starve it into surrendering Elisha to them. The "blindness" of the Syrians may have been due to their bewilderment at having lost all sense of direction; Elisha led them by unfamiliar tracks and byways, so confusing them until, terrified, they found themselves in the heart of Samaria. Elisha showed his servant—and this is a lesson for us too—that the "hosts of Yahweh" are a heavenly protection if only we have faith. The prophet may, of course, have used his hypnotic power on the will of the Syrian captain, whom the soldiers would follow as a matter of discipline. The clever ruse ended in a surprise feast for the Syrians, who returned more than ashamed at their experiences, and "came no more into the land of Israel" (2 Kings vi, 23).

Elisha still had the task of carrying out orders given by Yahweh to Elijah. First, at Damascus, he talked with Hazael, who was then on a mission from Ben-hadad, King of Syria; on his return Hazael rebelled and took the throne. His wars against Israel were fierce, but Elisha seems to have known they would be and regarded them as a means of bringing Israel to her senses.

Before he died Elisha told the king, Joash, to shoot his arrows eastwards towards Damascus, the capital of Syria: to do so was to declare war upon Syria. Later the king recovered his captured cities, as the prophet had said he would.

Prophecies Come True

The death of Ahab is told vividly in the Bible

Shalmaneser's Obelisk. It belongs to 860 B.C. and bears carvings and cuneiform writings about the king's conquests (p. 22).

story. Recent excavations in the city of Samaria have revealed much of the palace built by Omri and extended by Ahab. It was of yellow limestone, laid out with a central courtyard; in the rooms were housed the king's bodyguard and slaves, and in the stables were his magnificent war and chariot horses. The truth of the Bible story is borne out by the discovery of an artificial pool; this was probably the very one in which his servants washed Ahab's chariot and by which the pariah dogs gathered to lick at the blood-stained wheels.

Meanwhile, to complete his task, Elisha had persuaded Jehu to rebel against his king, Ahab's son. Jezebel, now an old woman, who had done so much harm with her false gods, was murdered, the pariah dogs pouncing madly upon her body, broken in its fall from the lattice window. The priests of Baal were slaughtered. By this terrible bloodshed Jehu drove out false idol-worship and returned the country to the worship of Yahweh.

A Dangerous Enemy

But it was not long before the Assyrian hordes were sweeping across the lands of Syria and Israel and threatening Judah. On the Black Obelisk of Shalmaneser (see 1 Kings xvi, 23) the cuneiform inscriptions and pictures include some of Jehu and Hazael, as well as the names of Ahab and Ben-hadad; it shows much of the history of this period (see also 1 Kings xx, 34 and xxii, 1). The record gives a vivid picture of Assyrian cruelty: "Karkar, his royal city, I destroyed, I devastated, I burned with fire. . . . I rained destruction upon them. I scattered their corpses far and wide . . . the plain was too small to let their bodies fall . . . with their bodies I spanned the Orontes (a river) as with a bridge." This was in 853 B.C., an important date for us, as it is the first date in our history of the Jews to be accepted as accurate by the majority of Biblical scholars; from this, other dates both before and after the Battle of Karkar may be calculated, although dates earlier than that of David—about 1000 B.C.—are difficult to fix with exactness.

Elisha to the very end was anxious that the king and the people should remain loyal to Yahweh, Who would save Israel from her enemies. But they did not learn their lesson either then or later.

Jewish captives being taken to the Assyrian king.

EXPRESSION WORK

1. In what ways did Elisha differ from Elijah? How were they alike?
2. Describe the strange departure of Elijah as seen by one of the prophet guild who followed the two prophets in secret.
3. Draw or model Elisha's "little room"; let the prophet thank his friends.
4. Prepare and act the scene in the cornfield.
5. Pretend you are Gehazi. Speak your thoughts aloud.
6. "The serving-maid has only one line to say, yet she is the chief character." What line is it?
7. What great modern doctor has done so much for lepers? Tell of his work, *or* prepare an article describing an interview with him.
8. Write a Radio Play on the story of Naaman.
   or
   Tell the story in strip cartoon.
   or
   Write a pen portrait or character sketch of Naaman.
9. You are the captain of the Syrian army. Report verbally to your king your experiences at Dothan.
10. Write out a sentence in the story of Elisha that seems to stand out as a special message.
11. How were Elisha's prophecies about Ahab and Jezebel fulfilled?
12. Mark on a map of Palestine all the places mentioned in this chapter and in the Bible references.

CHAPTER 4

AMOS

(Amos i, 1; ii, 6–8; iii; iv, 6–13; v, 4–15, 15–27; vi, 1–8; viii, 8–14; ix, 1–8)

IN 786 B.C. the King of Israel was Jeroboam II. Syria was at war with Assyria and Israel was free from attack for a number of years. She grew strong, her trade flourished and her power extended even to Damascus. For fifty years both Israel and Judah enjoyed peace and prosperity.

But, as in Solomon's time, power and trade brought luxury and splendour to the few and suffering and hardship to the many. The people kept their feast days and offered sacrifices and outwardly appeared to be serving Yahweh; but there was slavery, oppression and injustice that made their worship seem a mockery.

His Home Life

This is when we hear of Amos, the first of the Writing Prophets. He lived at Tekoa in Judah, about ten kilometres from Bethlehem. As a herdsman he looked after the hardy sheep that were able to exist on the thin scrubby grass of the Wilderness; these sheep produced a fine quality fleece, however, and at certain times of the year Amos would take his wool into the bigger cities of Bethel, Gilgal and Samaria to sell at the markets. At other times of the year he grew sycamore figs—fig-mulberries. These must not be confused with the fine figs with which we may be familiar. It is possible that Amos took to market branches and parts of the fig-tree, for fuel, altars, burnt-offerings, yokes and so on. The tree grows even today on the hill-slopes of this bleak district of Judah (Amos vii, 14).

It was a wild, desolate area; on three sides

A herdsman of today with his ass and flock. Amos was like this man.

23

Amos lived and worked in the Tekoan wilderness not far from these desert mountains, which gave him a deep sense of loneliness and awe at Yahweh's majesty.

the language of a shepherd, using his sling as had Jacob and David to guide his wandering sheep, carried his club to protect them, his rod to check them, sought and found water in the most unlikely places to refresh them.

In June he must have handed the care of his flock for a short time to a friend or relative, for he had to see to his sycamore trees. He then put on one side his staff, reed-pipe, sling, rod (club) and staff, and with only his flint knife in his girdle he set off. Probably a few score metres above the Dead Sea were small oases where the trees would grow; he would scramble down narrow gorges to reach them. The trees were often fifteen metres high, but their branches spread horizontally and offered easy movement for the agile Amos. It was tiring work, this "dressing", but it had to be done. Each fig was cut or pinched sufficiently to make it soft as the bitter juice was squeezed out; this encouraged the fruit to ripen more quickly, but as the crops were gathered by hand the work had to be done frequently. In the markets only the poor people bought these wild figs, so there was little profit.

reared grey limestone hills and to the east fell away 1,200 metres of lowlands, brown and parched; wild animals roamed by day and by night—wolves, jackals, panthers, leopards and hyenas. Amos scanned the wilderness around him and in its vastness saw the wonder of Yahweh; especially at night when the sky was bright with stars did he feel the majesty and might of the Creator; and by day when he caught glimpses of the water of the Dead Sea glinting in the hot sun, he must have felt that surely here must Yahweh reign.

His Work

His life was hard (see Ps. lxiii, 1). The scanty rain had barely fallen before hot suns dried the brooks into caked wadis; freshly springing flowers and grass quickly shrivelled under the heat; stony patches of ground seemed hardly worth the labour of tilling. Amos had learned to seek shelter for himself and his flocks; he spoke

A spray of figs. The fruit usually shows in April, at the time of Passover, but does not ripen until late summer.

A typical market scene of today. It is probably little different from what Amos saw in Samaria and Bethel.

To the City!

With this life behind him Amos felt strangely alone in the towns he visited to sell his wool and figs and wood. There was bustle and argument and noise; dogs, pigs, sheep, children fell over one another in anxiety and fear; women sat outside their mud-brick hovels grinding their corn, kneading dough and spinning wool or flax; some stood to talk, balancing gracefully on their heads pots of precious water fetched from the well outside the city walls. The men seemed to have more time; they filled the market-place at the entrance gate, talking over their business with gestures and much shaking of heads. A great deal of what he heard made Amos shudder. Who were these well-dressed men? Who were these ill-clad slaves cowering before them?

In the Market-place

He stood and watched the merchandise as it passed into the town on heavily-burdened mules, asses and oxen; the booths were stacked with wares—wool from Moab, tools, garments of sheepskin, goat- and camel-hair; jewellery from Egypt; perfumes, knives, swords, weights and measures from Damascus; Arabian spices; African ivory; gold from Ophir; vases from Greece; silver, pottery, ivory and silks from Phoenicia. Here there was wealth, but here, too, there was poverty. Amos reached the Temple with its four-pronged altar bearing smoking sacrifices; harps, flutes and timbrels echoed over the town; but the priests seemed not to be interested in their duties. The rich paid their dues with a swagger, then returned to make more money in the

The prophet saw women spinning. Look closely at the drawing and work out how it was done.

Call of Amos

Amos returned to Tekoa, but his mind was not on his sheep or his figs; it was on what he had seen and heard—on the scenes of cruel injustice he had found. But what could *he* do about it— he, a poor Judaean shepherd? Suddenly he knew? Yahweh was calling him; he was not trained as a prophet, he was not even a member of the prophet guilds—but he must go and speak out against these evils. Humble and uneducated though he was, he must become Yahweh's spokesman (iii, 8; vii, 15). Amos was stunned at the thought but knew it was true; and his spirit gave him power to do what Yahweh told him. And when he spoke it was with his Tekoan background behind him; his words, stern and simple, were vividly illustrated by his experiences and knowledge of country life—just as Jesus was to draw His lessons from everyday scenes of life in Palestine. Examples of this teaching are seen very clearly in iii, 4–8, 12; iv, 2, 13; v, 8; vi, 12; vii, 14; ix, 13.

"The Lord God (Yahweh) has spoken, Who can but prophesy?" Amos went to Samaria, the capital city. It was there that he heard of the approach of the Assyrians; he talked with the traders in the caravans from Damascus; they told him how the captured city had been foolish enough to rebel against her conquerors, who were even then advancing towards her gates once more

markets, and the poor found it well nigh impossible to get near the House of Yahweh at all.

When Amos moved to another part of the market the noise offended him even more. Frequently he heard the hoarse cry of a beggar and the shrill song of the water-carrier—"Ho, everyone who is thirsty!" But it was the cheating that horrified him—the use of false measures and weights below standard; mouldy and rotting corn being offered at prices the poor could not afford. He saw, too, moneylenders forcing the last coin of interest, rich men accepting children in payment for debts, men and women being bought by Philistine slave-traders, poor men fighting to the death for scraps of bread dropped near the baker's booth. Through the open courtyards of the big houses he could see the rich revelling in their luxuries (vi, 4, 6). The women, in their paint and perfume, encouraged their husbands in this selfish and cruel extravagance; as Amos looked at them he scornfully compared them with the "kine of Bashan" (iv, 1).

What was happening to the people of the Northern Kingdom? They were Yahweh's, as he of the Southern Kingdom was Yahweh's; they were all of the Promised Land, they were His chosen people; they were brothers—the rich *and* the poor.

Scarabs and an Egyptian amulet representing the sun-god, in precious stones and ivory. The Egyptians believed that the beetle (scarab) had the power of eternal life and wore these charms for protection against evil spirits.

One of the duties of the Priest was to offer sacrifice at the four-horned altar.

to subdue her utterly. It could not be long before Samaria, too, would be besieged; it was only a matter of time before the whole kingdom would be overrun—and defeat by the Assyrians would surely be punishment for Israel's wrong-doing, disobedience and injustice.

Amos Preaches

In Bethel Amos spoke sternly to the people; his message can be found in ii, 6–16. The rich, he said, were oppressing the poor, whose lives were now so cheap and worthless that they could be exchanged for the cheapest thing in any market—a pair of shoes (ii, 6; iv, 1; v, 11; vi, 4–6, viii, 6). Paying temple dues was not enough, attending services was not enough (v, 14 ff.); Yahweh could not, would not, accept their worship whilst there was cruelty; the "day of the Lord" for which they all hoped would never come whilst there was bitterness and bribery and slavery. They could not even be certain that Yahweh had no thought for any other nation; was He not Creator of the whole earth? (i, 3, 6, 9, 11, 13; ii, 1, 4, 6). Yet He must punish them for this wickedness as He had punished other nations. Syria had been punished, as had Ammon, Moab and Judah—and the people rejoiced. Now—Israel would suffer,

"For you sell good men for silver, the needy
   for a pair of shoes,
You trample on the heads of the weak and
   deny justice to the poor.
Above all nations I have blessed you with
   knowledge and freedom;
Therefore I will punish you for every last one
   of your sins!"

Amos had seen baskets of fruit, luscious summer fruits, in the courtyards of the rich—grapes, apricots, pomegranates, figs. Soon they would become over-ripe, unfit, dead. That would happen to Israel. He saw the workman handling his plumbline to test the straightness of a sloping wall, and told the people that Yahweh would test Israel for her uprightness too—"With a plumbline I am testing my people."

Amos is Stopped

Needless to say, this was not the kind of prophecy that the prosperous schemers wanted to hear. Even Amaziah at Bethel (vii, 10–13) missed the point of the prophet's words and declared him to be a plotter against the king, Jeroboam II. "Get back to your fellow-prophets," he sneered. Amos retorted that he was not one of those, nor even a seer; he was the spokesman of Yahweh, the Creator, the Lord of Hosts. Tradition says that Amos was beaten and thrown from the Temple courtyard and forbidden ever to preach there again. He then knew that to reach the people he must write his words; it is possible that some friendly scribe did this for him, which is why to this day we have his fiery words and reproaches in our Bibles.

Over his heavy white linen ephod, threaded with gold, blue and purple strands, Amaziah the High Priest slipped his blue linen robe with its border of embroidered pomegranates and tinkling golden bells. As he did so he may have thought more deeply about Amos. Passing over his head the jewelled breastplate, he may have paused to look at the gems that represented the ten tribes and to think wistfully of the other two tribes now divided from Israel. And he may have wondered if the division of the country meant that not only were the people separated from one another, but that they had drifted far from Yahweh Himself.

Amaziah did not dream then that within a few years Samaria would fall to the Assyrians as

To make sure the wall is upright, the builder uses a plumb-line (Amos vii, 7–9).

Amos had said it would, and that he, the High Priest, would—too late—regret his scorn of the prophet from Judah.

These weird shapes are filled waterskins. The water-carrier's occupation is despised, but he is always welcome in this hot country. Ps. cxix, 83 speaks of "a bottle in the smoke" and refers to the drying and tanning of a goat-hide over a smoky fire.

This is "Shoe Street". Every booth is a shoemaker's, even in modern times. Can you see the sandals and shoes?

EXPRESSION WORK

1. Was Amos a prophet? Why did he contradict Amaziah?
2. Prepare and act a dialogue between Amos and Amaziah.
3. Pretend you are Amaziah's messenger. Deliver a verbal message from the High Priest to King Jeroboam, about Amos.
4. Draw Amos with his sheep or by his trees.
5. Hosea must have known Amos. Let the two talk together in the market-place of one of the Northern Kingdom cities.
6. Suppose you are a trader. Give your news and views to Amos about the threat of Assyria. Use v, 27; vi, 7, 14; vii, 17.
7. Write out Amos v, 24. What was the background of these words?
8. Discuss how Amos came to the conclusion that God was a God of Justice.
9. Find the following references: Amos ii, 6, 8; iii, 10, 12, 15; iv, 1, 5; v, 12, 21–24; vi, 4–6, 11; vii, 12, 13; viii, 3, 5, 6, 10. List all the things against which Amos speaks, then rearrange them under three or four main headings.
10. Draw Amos dictating his message to a scribe. How did he become our first "written" prophet?
11. What is God's promise in ix, 13–15?
12. Amos drew lessons from everyday life. Give examples.

CHAPTER 5

HOSEA AND THE
FALL OF THE NORTHERN KINGDOM

(Hosea i, 1–3; ii; iii; iv; vi; viii, 4–6; xi; xiv, 1–8; the Exile—2 Kings xvii, 1–20, 24–29)

FOLLOWING the death of Jeroboam II there was strife, murder and bloodshed. Six kings came to the throne in quick succession, and of these four were conspirators and usurpers.

Call of Hosea

Hosea belonged to the Northern Kingdom; he was well-educated, friendly and human. As a boy he must have seen and heard Amos in the market-place of Bethel or Samaria. Amos had been roused by the injustices he saw—the unfairness between man and man—and he had preached that Yahweh was a just and righteous God. Hosea, whose ministry took place nearly a generation later, during the years 750–735 B.C., taught the lesson he learned bitterly in his own life.

Hosea's wife had left him and his three children. She sank eventually into squalor and even slavery; but Hosea loved her so much that when the chance came at the slave-market he bought her back. He paid fifteen pieces of silver and an omer (approximately three litres) of barley. Hosea saw his message in this. If he could love his wife so much that he forgave her, then Yahweh would forgive his beloved Israel. However low she sank He would take her back; He would be merciful if she repented and was sorry for what she had done. Note how like the message of the New Testament this is—that God is a Father, kind and loving.

Hosea was so much concerned with the fate of the people that he even gave to each of his children a name that carried a message; thus, Jezreel—to remind him of Jehu's massacres and bloodshed in Israel; Lo-Ruchamah—"for I will no more have pity on the house of Israel"—i.e. the unpitied one; Lo-Ammi—"for ye are not my people and I will not be your God"—i.e. not-

akin-to-Me. Eventually these names were changed —Jezreel to mean "God sows"; Ruchamah, pitied; Ammi, "My people".

His Message

Although he seems to have some close knowledge of the priesthood, Hosea's messages, like those of Amos, were built on things of the countryside that his hearers understood. Some

Look at this lad's face. Hosea may well have had this intent expression as he listened to Amos. Notice the scrip (wallet) on his belt.

30

Here is a baker. Look at the "loaves"—rather like flat pancakes. Hosea called Israel (Ephraim) "half-baked". What did he mean?

verses—e.g. ii, 22; v, 1; vi, 8 ff.—show how well he knew the landscape. He knew how the leopard prowled and then lay in wait for its prey, and saw Yahweh "like a leopard by the way I look for them (the sinful)", as a bear, as a lion, as a wildbeast (xiii, 5-9). There were rare occasions when Israel did obey the will of Yahweh, and then, Hosea said, "Your goodness is as a morning cloud, and as the early dew it goeth away." The Hebrew word for "dew" is the very lovely phrase "summer-sea-night-mist", referring to the misty fine rain that comes in from the Mediterranean in silvery clouds to freshen the countryside—a precious rain in times of drought.

In these passages Hosea shows how well he knew Samaria and Bethel—vii, 1; viii, 5; x, 5-7; iv, 15; x, 5; xii, 14. We read of their idolatry in ii, 8; iv, 13, 17; viii, 4-14; x, 8; xiii, 2; xiv, 8. His knowledge of farming is seen in iv, 16; viii, 7; x, 10 ff.; xiii, 3; vi, 3, 4; ix, 10; x, 1. Hosea reveals that he is well aware of the dangers of neighbouring countries and possible invasion, in such verses as v, 13; vii, 11; viii, 9; xii, 1. He spoke of Ephraim (Israel) as a "cake not turned" (vii, 8). His hearers knew what he meant: in their simple ovens they had often known how a cake could be burnt on one side and underdone on the other—

half-baked. Israel was neglecting one side of her life—the spiritual side (see vii, 4, 6, 7).

Hosea's messages were unpopular, of course, especially to the priests and the rich, who kept the poor in ignorance of the law and in poverty as well (iv, 6; xii, 7, 8).

Hosea announced that Israel would be devastated, and through her desolation and destruction would be made to realise that Yahweh did indeed love her; she would even be sent into captivity and exile, and her suffering would make her turn to Yahweh. His message is to a large extent contained in xi, 1-4 and xiv, 1-8.

Israel a "Buffer State"

Look again at your map and see how Israel lay between the great nations—Babylon and Assyria to the north and west, Egypt to the south—waiting for the chance to conquer the "buffer state", the land of trade and war routes. These three nations were watching each other like wild animals, waiting to attack. The whole of Palestine lay between them and complete power over their enemies. Already the land was divided within itself, torn by civil war, aggression and rivalry. Time and again its people had been invaded and countless numbers of them had been carried away. Now the might of Assyria was on the very

Tiglath-Pileser III, King of Assyria, in his chariot. Note especially the slave, the king, the harness and trappings.

borders of the Northern Kingdom. Like Amos, Hosea saw how dangerously near was the aggressor, and he knew that before long Samaria must fall a prey to the invader.

In about 738 B.C. King Menahem, in an effort to secure his own position as ruler, decided to pay tribute to Assyria, and sent to Tiglath-Pileser III one thousand talents of silver (a talent would be worth more than £500). But the enemy could not be bought off. Some of the king's courtiers advised friendship with Egypt, with gifts of olive oil, wood and wool. Hosea told them they were wasting their time and produce; the One to turn to before it was too late was Yahweh. . . . "Ephraim (Israel)," he said, "is like a silly dove, without understanding; to Egypt they cry, and hasten to Assyria. They strike bargains and carry oil to Egypt!" Hosea was reminding them of the Eastern proverb which says, "There is nothing more simple than a dove." Like the dove, Israel was heading for the snare (vii). Yet, if she would return to Yahweh and not trust in the idols of these countries, He would forgive her and look after her once more (xiv).

The Assyrians at War

Six years later, in 732 B.C., Tiglath-Pileser, having captured Gilead and Galilee, took Damascus, the great city of Syria. Five years later still the danger became very real; serious raids were made on Israel and captives were taken by the Assyrians. We shall hear much of these invaders, but we must try to picture them early in our story. They were warlike, cruel and determined; they showed no pity for their captives; they destroyed, burned all and spared none. Carvings in stone (called bas-reliefs) show them wearing long-fringed robes, usually tucked up or shaped to free their legs for movement in fighting; their long hair and square beards were closely curled and plaited; on their feet they wore leather sandals, on their heads helmets—probably of bronze. They carried bows and arrows and rode to the city walls on siege towers or tanks, from the tops of which—protected by wicker screens—they showered iron-tipped arrows upon the defenders of the city. On many of the bas-reliefs in the British Museum—and some of these are reproduced for you in the pictures in this

This bas-relief shows part of a battle in a forest. What are the soldiers doing? Look at their helmets and explain the difference between them.

book—you can see Tiglath-Pileser himself riding in his two-wheeled chariot. Some of his men are rearing a battering-ram from a kind of armoured lorry. The prisoners are also shown, some impaled on stakes, others roped together or falling prostrate before the Assyrians or bringing tribute and gifts of food and animals and golden vessels.

The Assyrians at Home

At home these people lived in luxury, for they were strong and powerful and demanded food, money and tribute of all kinds from the nations they conquered or frightened. Syria sent wood and bronze and articles made of these; Egypt sent gold, ivory, golden and jewelled vessels; Phoenicia sent dyes and silks and pottery.

Even when not fighting, the Assyrians spent much time in dangerous sports like wild bull and lion hunting; the king kept these animals in captivity so that they could be released for hunting at any time. Their god, Nergal, was a god of hunting and war; he is shown as having an Assyrian human head on the body of a four-footed animal—usually a bull or a lion. If you

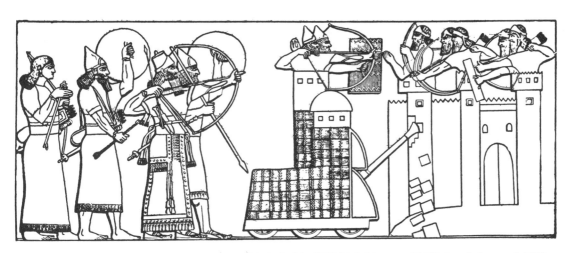

An Assyrian king before a besieged castle wall. Which is the king? Which is his servant? What are being carried? The battering-ram is breaking down the wall and the archers are high enough to attack the defenders.

Assyrian sport; hunting wild boar. You will see that the rider is sitting "side-saddle". Why?

look at the pictures you can see what huge figures these were. The drawing shows how each was moved by hundreds of workmen and slaves using ropes and the system of "levers and rollers". The Assyrians had other gods, like Nebo and Bel; these, too, were demanding of cruel worship (2 Kings xvii, 29). There is no doubt of the skill and power of these people; there is even less doubt of their bloodthirsty, cruel and swift conquests. And yet Israel hesitated.

Samaria Falls!

Some years later Shalmaneser decided to extend his kingdom to the Mediterranean. He demanded more tribute from Israel, who went on paying it for a time—and then refused. Shalmaneser promptly laid siege to Samaria. His successor, Sargon II, took over and after three years Samaria gave in; starved into surrender, her leaders opened the gates to the enemy (2 Kings xvii). The Assyrians loved to portray their conquests and to record their campaigns in their own wedge-shaped cuneiform script. Sargon wrote: "I besieged, took and captured the town of Samaria and carried into captivity 27,280 persons who lived in it."

The End of the Northern Kingdom

The Assyrians were utterly ruthless and believed in exterminating their conquered

peoples. Thus, we are told, the majority of the population of the Northern Kingdom were carried away beyond the Jordan to Nineveh in Assyria—never to return. Despite the warnings of Elijah, Elisha, Amos and Hosea, the "Lost Tribes" of Israel, as they are called, were gone for ever.

Sargon replaced the captives with those of other tribes he had conquered, and soon Samaria was occupied by strange people with strange tongues and strange idol-worship. These mixed races intermarried with those few Israelites left behind by Sargon; their descendants became the "Samaritans", of whom we shall hear more later.

From this time, 721 B.C., the Fall of Samaria, we are concerned no longer with the Northern Kingdom, for it ceases to exist; we follow now the fortunes—and misfortunes—of the Southern Kingdom, Judah, with her capital Jerusalem and her people the Jews.

The "Beginnings" of our Bible

This chapter has ended in the destruction of the Northern Kingdom, but it is as well for us to remember that from this sad end to Israel came a wonderful gift to the whole world. It is obvious that at least a few of the Israelites of the Northern Kingdom were anxious and able to flee the country in fear of the invading Assyrian army; they made their way to Judah in the south. They took with them precious manuscripts, the chronicles and stories of their land and ancestors, that were then being written down for fear they should be altogether forgotten. Scholars have since named these the E documents—E standing for Ephraim and Elohim, a Hebrew name for God in the Northern Kingdom. In the Southern Kingdom there were already in existence similar documents called J—standing for Judah and Jahveh, another spelling of Yahweh. These stories were similar to those of the Northern Kingdom, but differed in detail and style of writing. These two narratives of familiar stories were woven together in later years, and became the basis of our present Bible. You can trace these two different accounts in many of the early Bible stories, e.g. the Creation in Genesis i and ii, and the stories of Joseph, where the differences are indicated in Book I of this series, on p. 30.

Thus we owe the preservation of these wonderful stories to the refugees from the Northern Kingdom who brought for safe-keeping their precious documents; their loyalty to Yahweh brought for ageless possession the stories of the people and their God.

Nergal—the winged man-headed bull-god of the Assyrians.

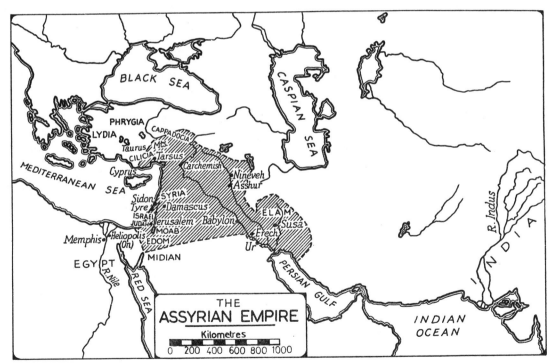

All the places mentioned in this account should be found on the map. Compare the size of the Assyrian Empire with that of each of the other great empires; the maps are on the same scale.

This shows how the massive bull-god was moved with rollers, ropes and levers by hundreds of slaves. Compare it with the moving of the Rameses statue in Book I, p. 46.

EXPRESSION WORK

1. Pretend you are Hosea, like the lad in the picture. What are you thinking about?
2. Write and act the scene in the slave-market when Hosea redeems (buys back) his wife.
    or
   What was the real significance of the strange names given to Hosea's children?
3. Compare the preachings of Amos and Hosea from the Bible references given; show how Hosea "echoed" Amos, then bring out the *new* ideas he developed.
4. Show on a map how Palestine, especially the Northern Kingdom, was a buffer state between Assyria and Egypt.
5. Why did Hosea speak of Ephraim as (*a*) a cake not turned, (*b*) a silly dove?
6. Copy or model on clay some of the bas-reliefs (pictures) of Assyrian soldiers.
7. Pretend you are a watcher on the walls of Damascus. Give to your anxious friends below reports of the invading Assyrians.
8. "I besieged, took and captured the town of Samaria." Let the king tell his admiring court about this conquest.
9. Model or draw an Assyrian winged bull-god.
10. From the drawing describe how the bull-god was moved into position by the use of ropes and "levers and rollers".
11. What are the "Lost Tribes"? Why are they so called?
12. Write and learn Hosea xiv, 9–11: "The ways ... in them."

CHAPTER 6

HEZEKIAH

(2 Kings xviii; xix; xx, 1–7; 2 Chron. xxix; xxx, 1–15; xxxii)

THE history of the Jews now centres in the Southern Kingdom of Judah. By the time Hezekiah came to the throne, about 725 B.C., there had been many bad and good kings. The "bad" kings were those who did "that which was evil in the sight of the Lord"—those who allowed and encouraged the worship of baals and idols and neglected Yahweh; the "good" kings were those who "did right in the sight of the Lord"—those who destroyed the groves, shrines and high places and insisted that Judah should worship Yahweh as the one true God of the people.

His Good Work

Hezekiah was a good king. He came to the throne a few years before the final attack of the Assyrians upon the Northern Kingdom. It must have seemed to him only a matter of time before Judah too would be invaded by the cruellest of all nations.

Judah itself lay to the east of the trade routes and could even be by-passed by marauding tribes and armies anxious to come to grips with one another for complete power; but Egypt to the south and Assyria to the north had no intentions of leaving Judah unconquered and possibly a thorn in their flesh. Besides, Uzziah had made the country prosperous once more and it was now a kingdom worth capturing for its own wealth.

The father of Hezekiah, Ahaz (not to be confused with Ahab of the Northern Kingdom), had been an idol-worshipper; he believed that the Syrian gods—like Reshef pictured on p. 38—could help him. When he was sent for to pay homage to Sargon he not only accepted his enemy but also his enemy's gods. On his return to Jerusalem he erected an altar like the one he had seen at Damascus, showing that he would pay tribute to Assyrian gods as well as to the Assyrian king. This would have meant a return to child-sacrifice too. Hezekiah cleared away this altar and all others used for the worship of false

The countryside of Judah, with its terraced slopes and fertile valleys. Not far away are the wilderness and rough hill-country and desert.

37

The Syrian storm-god Reshef in bronze and also carved on an Egyptian relief. How do you account for the same god being in two different countries? On the carving it says, "Reshef, god of the wind, the Great One, may he give you light and life every day."

gods; he had the Temple cleansed, reopened and reconsecrated. The people welcomed these changes, sudden as they were, and Hezekiah decided to celebrate Passover, which had been neglected since the time of Solomon. You can read about Passover in Book I. The feast was held to remind the Jews of the last meal the Children of Israel had had before their release from Egyptian slavery. Invitations were sent through the length and breadth of the land—"from Dan to Beer-sheba"—and by so doing Hezekiah was trying to bring the people back to Yahweh. It is probable that Isaiah helped him to word the invitations. Read what he said in 2 Chron. xxx, 6–9. It is sad to find that so many of the tribes "laughed them to scorn and mocked them". But the feast was attended by many loyal Jews and lasted for fourteen days instead of seven.

The Serpent of Brass made by Moses in the Wilderness and kept in the Temple held some strange attraction for the people, and for many of them was an object of worship and a symbol of Yahweh. Hezekiah felt this was wrong and had it destroyed, for to him it was merely "Nehustan"—a piece of brass.

Safeguarding the Water-supply

By now Israel, the Northern Kingdom, had fallen and the frontiers of Judah stood as a final challenge to the conquering Assyrians. Hezekiah knew the danger, and having repaired the Millo earthworks built by David and strengthened by Solomon, turned his attention to one of the key factors of an army's existence in the land—the water-supply. If he could cut off or diminish that he might stave off invasion. Asking, "Why should the kings of the Assyrians find much water?" he and his people set about the control of all water-supplies, fountains and streams. There are references to this in 2 Chron. xxxii, 4; 2 Kings xx, 20; Isa. xxii, 9.

Excavations have revealed his wonderful feat of engineering. Look at the picture of the entrance to the cave, how forbidding it is. You will remember that wells were much more often than not outside the city walls, whence the women fetched water in pots and jars and skins, and where the shepherds watered their flocks more easily because there was more room than in the city itself. Other water-supplies within the city were available, of course. Hezekiah had dug a tunnel from Gihon, the Virgin's Spring, where the natural spring supply was, through 530 metres of solid rock. It led into the Pool of Siloam. Evidently dug in a hurry, it is not by any means

Here is the entrance to Hezekiah's tunnel, described on this page. It was discovered some years ago by two boys.

a perfect piece of work, being uneven and unequal. But it does represent a remarkable task, for, boring from opposite ends, the workmen met almost exactly as planned. Here is part of the inscription cut in the rock: "While yet they plied the drill, each towards his fellow . . . there was heard the voice of one calling unto another . . . on the day of the boring through the stonecutters struck, each to meet his fellow, drill upon drill, and the water flowed from the source to the pool for a thousand and two hundred cubits." (Remember that a cubit was 46 to 51 centimetres.) The outer end of the tunnel—shown in the picture—was disguised and hidden so that the Assyrians would not find it. It was rediscovered in A.D. 1880 by two inquisitive and adventurous boys.

Hezekiah's Foolishness

Soon after this work was completed, Hezekiah fell desperately ill. He probably had some poisonous abscess which, neglected, would prove dangerous. It is at this time that we meet Isaiah, of whom we have so far heard little. He treated the king's illness with a poultice of figs; an ancient remedy for a sick horse, it certainly cured Hezekiah.

The king recovered and received gifts and kind greetings from no less a person than the prince of Babylon. Hezekiah was delighted and invited him to Jerusalem, where he was shown the king's treasures and the wealth of the Temple. This was an unwise, even a foolish, thing to do. Babylon was an enemy to Assyria and might prove a welcome friend to Judah, but having seen all the splendour of Judah the prince was sure to report to his father, who might decide that Judah was worth capturing too. Isaiah (xxxix, 6) reproved Hezekiah for his lack of foresight.

The Threat of Sennacherib

Meanwhile the Assyrians were getting uncomfortably nearer. Isa. x tells vividly how swiftly Sennacherib moved westwards, conquering as he came; one after another the little kingdoms fell, until in Judah itself forty-six cities, including Lachish, were taken by storm. A tremendous tribute was demanded from Hezekiah, who had to strip his palace and the Temple of all their gold and rich hangings to meet it; he even

Assyrian archers behind a screen of wickerwork—interlaced reeds strengthened with leather. What is each doing?

gave up a captured Philistine king as part of the ransom. Like other kings, Sennacherib recorded his campaigns on his own cylinder of baked clay. This is now in the British Museum, and is called the Taylor Prism; on p. 62 of Book I is a copy of part of the account of the siege of Jerusalem, in cuneiform script. On one part of the six-sided cylinder are these words: "As for Hezekiah, King of Judah, who did not submit to my yoke, forty-six of his strong-walled cities I besieged by escalade, by bringing up siege engines, by storming, by mines, tunnels and breaches. I took two hundred thousand people . . . horses, mules, asses, camels, cattle and sheep. . . . As for Hezekiah himself, I shut him up in Jerusalem, his royal city, liked a caged bird. . . . The Arabs and his mercenary soldiers . . . deserted him. Thirty talents of gold, eight hundred talents of silver, gems, antimony, jewels, precious stones, ivory couches and chairs, elephants' hide, ivory, maple, cedar . . . his daughter, his harem and his musicians, he had them brought after me to Nineveh, my royal city."

Assyrian Warfare

There is no doubt that he launched his attack from Lachish, which he had made his headquarters and centre from which to control the way to Egypt as well as to Jerusalem. Lachish has been excavated and has revealed many historical facts. The bas-reliefs showing the siege —that once adorned the palace at Nineveh, the capital of Assyria—are now in the British Museum. (See 2 Kings xviii, 14, 17; xix, 8; Isa.

Here is an Assyrian siege-engine followed by spearmen. Compare the helmets and armour of the fighters. What is the front man doing?

xxxvi, 2.) These show thirteen slabs carved with scenes from the siege, the assault and capture of the city of Lachish, the prisoners and plunder. The title reads: "Sennacherib, the mighty king of the country of Assyria, sitting on the throne of judgment, before the city of Lachish. I give permission for its slaughter."

Attack!

What had happened at Lachish now seemed likely to happen at Jerusalem. The Assyrians set up mounds of mudbricks, soil, rocks and trees; up these were to be rushed the siege-engines or battering-rams. These were mounted on four wheels and were leather-covered for the protection of the invaders—three in each, one to handle the ram, one to shoot iron-tipped arrows, one to put out fire-brands hurled from above by the defenders on the city walls. Looking closely at the bas-reliefs you can see kneeling archers backed by rows of standing men, protected by others holding shields of leather-covered wicker-work. The Assyrian bowmen wear conical peaked helmets, but those of the shield-bearers and spearmen have crests or combs not unlike those on firemen's helmets.

There are slingers and spearmen, horsemen, charioteers. The prisoners are pathetically kneeling—men, women and children, even babies. The king sits on his rich throne, his feet on a stool, in his right hand two arrows, on his left a bow. A slave carries his parasol to protect him from the sun. The slave in a turban is cleanshaven and is probably a Canaanite; the Assyrians themselves all have long, square-cut beards, their long hair curled at the ends; the Judaeans wear short, curled beards, more rounded at the corners, and their hair is curled all over the head. The landscape is indicated by olive and fig trees and clusters of grapes.

Surrender!

Hezekiah knew what to expect and the murderous revenge likely to befall him for his refusal to give in. Probably Sennacherib, with his eyes on Egypt as well, did not want to risk either

Slingers. They hurled great stones over the walls of the besieged city with remarkable skill and accuracy.

Some of the Jewish defenders. What are they doing? How do they differ from the Assyrians?

losing too many men or a stab in the back from Egypt. So he sent someone to try and talk the king into surrender.

Acting on Isaiah's advice, Hezekiah told the people in the city that Yahweh would save them. The Assyrian chief officer, the Rabshakeh, came to the walls and shouted up to the besieged people. He accused them of trusting Egypt— "this bruised reed" (2 Kings xviii, 21). Read his speech aloud and see how full of taunts, flatterings and accusations it is; see how cunning and furious he is at getting no answer to his bluff— especially when he jibes that he will provide two thousand horses if the king can produce the riders. Hezekiah had already asked Egypt for cavalry! The Rabshakeh's threat that they would

die of thirst and famine was wasted on the Jews as they thought of their strategy in securing a safe water-supply. The nations the Rabshakeh mentions were some of those overrun by the Assyrians on their way to Palestine; many of the captives had been deported to other lands, just as had been those of the Northern Kingdom.

The chief officer returned to Sennacherib, who advanced his army up the slope towards the city walls; he brought up his deadly siege-engines, began piling up the mounds near the walls and lined up his men according to the weapons they used. Before long, thought the fearful watchers, it would be Lachish all over again; not even Yahweh could save them now. Still Sennacherib hesitated; his main army was towards Egypt— ought he to attack? He wrote to Hezekiah. Surrender—or . . .! Hezekiah then did a wise thing; he talked to Yahweh about it. You will find his fine prayer in 2 Kings xix, 15–19. Isaiah gave his good advice, for he was quite sure that Yahweh would save Jerusalem, even at this late hour. Isaiah had, of course, previously told the king not to break with Assyria, but once the king had done so the prophet remained loyal to him. Remembering that the sign of Assyria was a fierce bull, he said that "this raging bull shall be tamed and driven back", with a rope through the ring in its nose! In other words, the Assyrians would never succeed in their siege of Jerusalem.

King Sennacherib is receiving tribute from the Jews of conquered Lachish. Having taken Lachish he turned his attention to Jerusalem. Who are the kneeling figures?

Part of a bas-relief from Sennacherib's palace. His Cylinder, 686 B.C., is a six-sided cylinder of baked clay recording the campaigns of the king, including the siege of Jerusalem. Part of the cuneiform script is shown in Book I, p. 62.

Destruction of Sennacherib

That night the Assyrians were pitched against the city walls; the blow would fall at any moment, perhaps that night. It did—but not against Jerusalem. A strange event took place in the besieging army. No one is quite sure what it was; some say a plague broke out, brought and spread by hordes of field-mice (rats and mice do spread diseases); they even gnawed through the bow-strings of the bowmen. In the morning light the anxious defenders saw the army—dead. To the Jews this Assyrian disaster could mean only one thing—Yahweh's Angel of Death had passed over the camp (Isa. xxxvii; 2 Kings xix). Dismayed by this unexpected catastrophe, with his army weakened and Egypt near enough to make a decisive attack, Sennacherib retired and made his way back to Nineveh. His famous records say: "As for Hezekiah himself, the fear of my royal armies cast him down"; but there is no reference to his failure to take Jerusalem!

The city was saved once again and her people felt rather more secure than they might have done could they have known what the future held for them. Many believed that after this great escape Jerusalem would never fall to a conqueror; they did not foresee the victorious armies of—Babylonia, whose prince had seen the treasures of the palace and the Temple a few years before.

EXPRESSION WORK

1. "Hezekiah was a good king." What does this mean?
2. Reword Hezekiah's letter in modern English.
3. Discuss the water-supply of Jerusalem from the point of view of the king and his advisers.
4. Tell the story of the discovery of Hezekiah's tunnel as one of the two boys may have told it.
5. Pretend you are workmen within a few feet of meeting each other from opposite ends of the tunnel. Act the final meeting.
6. As prince, report to your father, the King of Babylonia, about your visit to Hezekiah, King of Judah.
7. Find out all you can about Lachish. Prepare to give a talk on this ancient city. Drawings and pictures will help.
8. Find and learn Byron's poem "Destruction of Sennacherib", and check against the Bible references.
9. What lesson might we learn from Hezekiah's trust in Yahweh?
10. Read 2 Kings xiv, 22; xv, 1–7; 2 Chron. xxvi, 1–15, and draw a map to show the extent of Uzziah's kingdom inherited by Hezekiah.
11. As a watchman on the wall of Jerusalem, give a report of the Rabshakeh, the preparation for assault, the strange withdrawal and the scene on the next morning.
12. Act or write the dialogue between Sennacherib and the king bringing tribute—as shown in the picture.

CHAPTER 7

ISAIAH, MICAH, JOSIAH

(Isa. i, 1–20; ii; v, 1–24; vi, 1–13; vii, 1–7; ix, 2, 6, 7; x, 20–24; xi, 1–9; xxviii, 23–29;
xxxi, 6; xxxv, 3–10; xxxvi; xxxvii. Micah ii, 1–3, 8–11; iii, 1–8; vi, 6–12; vii, 1–7. 2 Kings
xxi, 1–6, 16; xii; xxiii, 1–8)

ISAIAH

WITHOUT Isaiah, Hezekiah would probably have given in to Sennacherib and failed in his kingship. Who, then, was Isaiah? And why had he such a fine influence upon the king?

It is not easy to find this merely by reading the book bearing his name. For one thing, scholars tell us that not all the book was written by one man, but that there were probably three authors; also, the chapters are not in chronological order, so the prophecies do not follow one another correctly. But Isaiah was certainly an historical character, a real person. His call to serve Yahweh and be a spokesman is given in chapter vi, 1–13; he had most to do between the years 740–700 B.C. Isaiah himself was unlike any of the prophets of whom we have already heard. They were of ordinary birth and background. Isaiah was a statesman, well-educated, rich, familiar with the king's court, and adviser to Hezekiah.

Isaiah the Statesman

Isaiah knew of the dangers arising from military alliances and did not want Judah dragged into war. Ahaz, King of Judah, was being encouraged to join the Syrian and Israelite kings in fighting the Assyrians; these two kings even attacked Jerusalem in an attempt to force him; but Ahaz wanted to "buy" help from the very enemy who swept over the other two countries and was left to pay (2 Kings xvi, 7). Isaiah said this was foolish but Ahaz ignored him. When, in the same way years later, Hezekiah wanted to buy help from Egypt, Isaiah advised him against that too. The prophet said, "Keep away from these warring nations; stay neutral."

Isaiah must have seen this view many times; it is one approach to the city of Jerusalem.

The story Isaiah told in his "Song of the Vineyard" was a familiar one to his hearers. Compare this drawing with the photograph on p. 14.

Not only was this wise for political reasons (xx; xxi, 1) but also from the religious point of view. Other gods had failed their nations but Yahweh would save Judah, for He was in the Temple at Jerusalem, the City of God; this would prove Him to be the one true God.

His Call

The prophet had felt his unworthiness (vi), but his "Here am I; send me" gave him great courage and confidence. He had received his call in the Temple itself, whilst in some kind of trance. What impressed Isaiah most was the holiness of God. He felt sure that his country would one day fall to an invader, and his message therefore centred on the "remnant of Israel" who were to be a holy people serving a Holy God.

"Song of the Vineyard"

This belief sent him out to do God's work— to forth-tell. It was probably at a vintage festival when the people were happily celebrating the year's good grape-harvest that he sang his song of the vineyard (v, 1–7). He sang as a minstrel and the people gathered round him. He told of the preparation of the vineyard, in a sunny spot and in fertile soil. The vineyard was cultivated by hand, since a plough could not be used on the hill-slope, and the stones were cleared away; strong plants were put in. Next came protection —a watch-tower such as that used by Naboth to look over his vineyard, a hedge and a stone wall to keep out thieves and goats; and a vat was hewn out of the limestone for the grape-trampling at harvest time. But the harvest failed, and there grew only wild, sour grapes. Here Isaiah turned to his hearers and there was a change of rhythm in his song. Judge, he said, what should be done. The vineyard must be destroyed. Down must come the hedge and the wall; the cattle and goats should devour the vines. The vineyard must be left to rot and shrivel, untended, unpruned, undug. Ah, sang Isaiah, "the vineyard of the Lord of Hosts is the house of Israel, the men of Judah His pleasant plant; and He looked for judgment, but behold oppression; for righteousness, but behold a cry." In the original Hebrew tongue the prophet makes a play on words here; he meant, "He looked for rule and found misrule; for redress and behold distress."

The people had condemned themselves; they were indeed a neglected vineyard that should be destroyed. Yet, said Isaiah, a few should be saved—a remnant to whom Yahweh's majesty and holiness would be powerful guides for living.

Isaiah even called his son Shear-Jashub, meaning "a remnant shall return to God".

Warning!

On another occasion, Isaiah carried around with him a kind of notice-board or poster; it was a clay tablet bearing the words MAHER-SHALAL-HASH-BAZ, which meant "swift-spoil-speedy-prey". He was trying to make it clear that Judah would one day be the prey of the swift Assyrians; he gave this strange name to his second son.

To Isaiah the promise of a Messiah was to be the reward of the "chosen people", the remnant. His words are familiar to us as part of the Christmas story and in Handel's *Messiah*. Note especially ix, 1–7 and xi, 1–9. Amos had seen Yahweh as a God of justice, Hosea as a God of love; Isaiah was positive that He was a God of righteousness and holiness, Who would accept nothing that was wicked or impure. To this end He would forgive (i, 18), if they would but give up their sins, injustices and idol-worship. . . . "His hand is stretched out still."

"A Lodge in a Garden"

There came a time when there was much distress and confusion in Jerusalem. News of disasters came in daily; refugees crowded into the city, workmen strengthened the walls and prepared to secure the water-supplies; beaten soldiers straggled back with their vivid stories of defeat and death at the hands of the invaders. Not a few people flocked to the Temple in their panic and anxiety; others were reckless and carefree, seeking what they thought to be their last pleasures before the siege of the city and its fall. Isaiah watched all this; in imagination he saw the victorious armies conquering village after village and city after city in their advance upon Jerusalem, left isolated "as a booth in a vineyard, as a lodge in a garden of cucumbers" (i, 8). The prophet recalled the booths or shelters of brushwood and branches built on the hill-slopes during the Feast of Tabernacles; he knew too of the even more flimsy and loosely-made shelters that the worker made for himself in the fields or vineyard or orchard for protection against the rain and sun. There is a picture of one in Book I on page 76. Such structures were left until they fell to pieces in the rain and wind, when they presented pictures of ruin and desolation. That was how "the daughter of Zion" would be left because Jerusalem had disobeyed Yahweh. Yet Yahweh would lop down their enemies as a woodman cut down trees—if the people would heed his words. But his words fell on deaf ears.

The wine-press, hewn out of stone or built like this one. The weight at the end of the bar caused the rock beneath it to crush the grapes; the juice ran into a trough, was collected and poured into large pottery jars.

Isaiah's Message

His message was one of confidence and hope and trust (xxxi, 15). Just as Amos had done, he said he was certain that Yahweh would look after any nation with real faith in Him (xxvi, 2), and that other nations might be His instruments (viii, 7 and x, 5), despite their power to conquer (x, 15 and xxxvii, 29). Amos had pointed out the folly of lip-service and mere ritual in worship; Isaiah now said that what God really wanted from everybody was righteousness, charity and fair-dealing (i, 11–18: compare Ps. li). Like Amos, too, he was angry at social wrongs, especially those brought on by the luxury-loving women. Amos had called them cows of Bashan (iv, 1); Isaiah has a bitter passage about them too (iii, 18). There were other injustices towards the poor (iii, 14 and v, 8, 9).

His Advice

Like the prophets before him, Isaiah tried to help his hearers by referring to things they knew about. Thus, in xxviii, 23–29, there is an excellent description of farming; in xvii, 6 and xxiv, 13, he talks of the olive berries left on the tree after the beatings at harvest and compares them with the "remnant" of holy people. He mentions the potter in xxix, 16 and xxx, 14; the "potter's vessel beaten down" refers to the crushing of broken pottery to powder for making cement. When a pot is broken in the home the larger pieces are saved for "taking fire from the hearth", as we might use a dustpan; curved pieces called "sherds"—hence, "pot-sherds"—were laid beside the well or brook so that thirsty travellers could use them for scooping up water to drink. The prophet says that the crushing of Yahweh's disobedient people would be final and total destruction—like the grinding to powder of the pieces of the potter's vessel (compare Jer. xix, 11).

Isaiah refers to homely things like using a razor (vii, 20); robbing birds' nests (x, 14 and xvi, 2); beds too short for comfort (xxii, 18); faithfulness like a firm nail (xxii, 23). Note how clearly these references must have carried messages if only the people had bothered to think about them. When they jibed at him he retorted that they would be taught in a foreign tongue—the tongue of the invader (xxviii, 9–13). His words about molten and graven images—those made in the melting pot and those carved from stone—remind us that false worship was still common in the land; the people were loth to give up the gods that they

Gathering olives. The tree was shaken and beaten by women and boys. The olives were crushed in the press for their oil (Book I, p. 74).

The potter's work is much the same in many Eastern countries. He works the bottom wheel with his feet and the top one spins; with his free hands he shapes his jars and bakes them hard in a nearby oven.

could see, in order to trust in a God they could not see.

What happened to this great statesman-prophet? Tradition tells us that by the Pool of Siloam he was hideously murdered—what Heb. xi, 37 describes as "sawn asunder"—by the evil king Manasseh, in whose reign Judah returned once more to her sinful and wicked ways.

MICAH

Micah was a contemporary of Isaiah; that is, he lived at about the same time; his preaching covers the years 715–701 B.C. Because of the power and work of Isaiah, Micah was to some extent overshadowed by his older friend, although some of his messages were at times identical with those of Isaiah. This you can see if you compare, for instance, Isa. ii, 2–4 with Mic. iv, 1–3. None the less, Micah had much to say about Judah's religion and fate. He, too, complained of injustices (ii, 2 and iii, 10); about the greed of the wealthy (ii, 1–4 and iii, 1); about mere lip-service in worship (vi, 6–8; iii, 11 and iv, 3, 4).

One hundred years after he had made his prophecy about Jerusalem in iii, 12, his words were repeated by Jeremiah (xxvi, 18, 19). The book bearing his name is probably a collection of prophecies by at least three writers, but contains some fine passages and noble thoughts. Chapters i–iii are Micah's, iv and v relate to a later period; vi and vii refer to the Babylonian captivity rather than to the Assyrian conquest.

The Prophet's Background

Little is known of the prophet; he was born at Moresheth, a village in the Shephelah district near the Philistine border, thirty kilometres west of Tekoa, the home of Amos. He must have watched the caravans along the trade route to Egypt and he had seen too often the armies of the invaders; obviously country-bred, he saw and knew of the oppression and starvation of the poor—he saw it in Judah as Amos had seen it in Israel. He heard about the destruction of Damascus and Samaria and knew that Jerusalem would eventually fall because of her social wrongs. Strangely enough, he has little if anything to say about false idol-worship; he seems more concerned with justice.

He knew that some of the rich landowners stole their poorer neighbours' ground by moving landmarks and boundary stones; no one could prove that the stones had been moved and the wealthy farmers gained by this cheating. They even lent to their victims the corn grown on this stolen land and charged such a high rate of interest that when the farmers could not pay they had to give up the rest of their little farms: some

Isaiah poured much scorn on Judah's false idols (Isa. ii, 8). The bird-faced one was made by hand in Mesopotamia, but was found in Palestine. The "mother-goddess" has a feathered headdress and is Canaanite; how do you know it was cast in a mould?

had to give themselves when their property was gone, and they and their families became servants and slaves to their rich cheating neighbours.

Micah watched the oxen trample corn on the threshing-floor and felt that Jerusalem would one day be trampled by a powerful enemy.

But the prophet preached a message of hope and peace and joy in the land; and, like those prophets who had before him said similar things and given the same warnings, Micah was laughed at by the very people he most wanted to help.

JOSIAH

Manasseh—a Bad King

On the death of Hezekiah, Manasseh—an evil king—came to the throne and once more encouraged idol-worship. He was only twelve years of age, so the responsibility really falls upon the shoulders of those ruling for him; but as he grew older he continued their wrong-doing and rebuilt the high places, shrines and altars. He even introduced sun, moon and star worship; he paid tribute to Assyria and took over the Assyrian gods. The chief of these was Astarte (called Ishtar by the Babylonians), the Mother-goddess of these Eastern nations. She was often called the "Queen

of Heaven", and all sorts of cruel sacrifices, mainly of children, together with superstitious beliefs, were connected with the worship of this goddess. Shamash, another god, was supposed to ride in a horse-drawn chariot, for he was the sun-god; his chariot was placed in the Temple itself. In place of the prophets and priests, Manasseh had sorcerers and wizards; he persecuted and murdered all believers in Yahweh that he could find; Isaiah was one of these. In 2 Chron. xxxiii, 12, 13, and in the Apocrypha, is the Prayer of Manasseh, which some writers say proves the king's final repentance for all his wrong-doing; but history does not agree and what 2 Kings xxi, 16 says is probably more true.

Josiah—a Good King

It is good to know that his grandson Josiah, only eight, next became king, ruling from 639 to 608 B.C. He was a good king, guided by better advisers and faithful followers of Yahweh. Once again, like Hezekiah, he set about ridding the country of idols and worship of false gods. The power of Assyria was waning and this made his reforms the easier to carry out. Again the Temple was cleansed and repaired; money for this was collected and spent on the wages of carpenters and masons, as well as for their materials—timber from Lebanon and stone from the quarries of Solomon.

A Great Discovery

It was when cleaning out rooms and wall niches that Hilkiah the High Priest made his startling discovery of a roll of the scriptures which had most probably been hidden during the persecutions of Manasseh's cruel reign. This roll is believed to have been part of the Book of Deuteronomy; even in those days such a roll would be a great treasure. Shaphan, a scribe whose duty it was to keep copies of the scriptures, took it to Josiah, who read the words now to be found in Deut. xxviii, 1–6, 15–17. He was horrified at what the words of the Law of Moses revealed; Judah had indeed sunk low, she had forgotten her holy Covenant (Deut. xxvi, 16–19).

Repentance and Reform

Josiah rent his robe and put on sackcloth and ashes upon his head; this was the usual sign of grief and sorrow. He sent for advice and Huldah, a prophetess, brought him messages from Yahweh. She told him that for her sins Jerusalem would be punished by captivity, but he, Josiah, would be spared that disgrace in his own reign. The roll was read to the people, who agreed to reform. As a sign of their conversion they destroyed everything connected with false idol-worship—the idols, shrines, vessels, the horses and chariots of the sun-god, the pole Asherah, altars. . . . These were burned or broken to pieces by the Brook Kedron outside the city. An order went out that from then on sacrifice was to be made in Jerusalem and nowhere else, and all village sacrifice had to cease. Then, like Hezekiah, Josiah called for a celebration of the Passover for rededication (see Deut. xii, 1–7). It is helpful to note here that Deuteronomy contains the words of Moses spoken during his last days before the Israelites crossed the Jordan, together with a collection of laws. The book teaches that God expects us to love and respect our neighbours as ourselves—the teaching of Jesus Himself. We should remember, too, how much Jesus used the words of Deuteronomy, especially in His Temptations and also in His teachings—e.g. Matt. iv, 1–11, especially verses 4, 7, 10.

Fall of Nineveh

Meanwhile a new threat was clearly on the way, this time from Egypt. To the far north Scythian hordes had swept in their fierce attacks across the Fertile Crescent, and had taken heavy toll of the power of Assyria. Assyria was weakening and could not face up to these new attacks and hold on to her many conquests as well. In 612 B.C. the capital city Nineveh fell. You will find that chapter iii of the little book of Nahum is a whoop of joy at this event; part of it in modern translation says:

"Hark to the whips, to the rumbling of wheels;
  Horses are prancing,
  Chariots leaping,
  Cavalry charging;
  Swords flash like flames and spears as the
    lightning;
  There's abundance of slain and a mass of
    dead bodies;"

—a vivid description of the kind of bloodshed the Assyrians had in former battles brought upon other nations.

In the mason's yard today, cutting and shaping stone for building much as it was done in the time of Isaiah.

Death of Josiah

Egypt, strangely enough, was moving northwards in an effort to help Assyria; perhaps she was anxious about the possible downward sweep of those Scythian marauders. At Megiddo, where

A Roll of the Law. Hilkiah found one and brought it to Josiah.

This is modern Nineveh, the capital of what was Assyria. In the foreground excavations of the ancient city are being made. Nahum rejoiced at its fall in 612 B.C.

Solomon had had his stables in days gone by and where Sisera had been routed by Deborah and Barak, Josiah was executed as a suspected and disloyal vassal. 2 Kings xxiii, 28–37 gives a different impression that is not confirmed by Egyptian records. Pharaoh Necho put a new king over Judah, but three years later was himself defeated by the Babylonians in a decisive battle at Carchemish, in 605 B.C. (Jer. xvi, 2).

By this time all Josiah's good work was undone. It was now the turn of yet another prophet to sound the alarm. This he could do with a great deal of experience behind him. He had heard of the attacking Scythians when he was but a youth; news of the fall of Nineveh came to Jerusalem at the time he began his preaching and prophecy; he knew full well that before he became an old man he would see the fall of his beloved city of Jerusalem unless . . . So he, too, warned his people; and they laughed at him as they had always done. The name of this prophet is Jeremiah.

EXPRESSION WORK

1. Why does Isaiah's call to serve Yahweh appear so late in his book (chapter vi)? How does it compare with the visions of Ezekiel i, 26–28; Amos ix, 1; Moses, Ex. xxiv, 9–12?
2. Describe or draw a street scene in Jerusalem in 740 B.C. *or*
   Prepare 2 Kings xviii–xix and Isa. xxxvi–xxxvii for Dramatic Reading in Morning Assembly.
3. *Girls:* Pretend you are ladies of the court and discuss Isaiah's denouncement in Isa. iii.
   Boys: Pretend you are their husbands and discuss the same passage.
4. Select some records of Handel's *Messiah* that contains words of Isaiah. Find the words, then play the records.
5. Make a model of "a lodge in a garden" and place a clay figure under it (Isa. i, 8).
6. Prepare and act scenes between Ahaz and Isaiah and Hezekiah and Isaiah in which the prophet warns each king not to side with enemy nations.
7. Make a poster to represent Isaiah's clay tablet bearing the words MAHER-SHALAL-HASH-BAZ. What do they mean?
8. How did Isaiah make the people condemn themselves in his parable of the vineyard (Isa. v)?
9. How do Isaiah ii, 2–4 and Micah iv. 1–4 compare? Write and act a dialogue between these two prophets.
10. "There is a remnant that bears the seed of promise" (Isa. vi). What does this mean? Did Isaiah realise his failure from the start or was he hopeful of success? What made him decide to preach, whatever the result?
11. Read Isa. viii, 17–18. Choose a group as the "guild of prophets" and discuss Isaiah's future work and plans.
12. Write and act the scene of the discovery of the Roll.

CHAPTER 8

JEREMIAH AND THE FALL
OF THE SOUTHERN KINGDOM

(Jer. i, 1–15; v, 1–6, 15–19, 25–30; vii, 1–15, 21–24; xviii, 1–12; xx, 1–6; xxii, 13–19; xxiii, 5–8; xxiv, 1–10; xxvi, 1–16; xxviii; xxxi, 29–34; xxxiv; xxxvi, 1–32; xxxvii, 11–21; xxxviii, 1–13; xxxix, 1–10. Lam. i)

JEREMIAH was born in about 650 B.C. at Anathoth, just to the north-west of Jerusalem, on the edge of the wilderness, where he learned what it was to experience intense heat and bitter cold, darkness and light, rain and drought, famine and plenty, danger and safety. All these experiences are seen in his teachings and preachings, for like the prophets before him, as a prophet-spokesman of God he explained things to the people in parables and events that were familiar to them. Like most of the prophets, he did not want to answer his call; he was timid and gentle, and shrank from the task of speaking in public against the wrongs he saw.

"Wake Up!"

Early in his book we find him looking at the beautiful almond tree in blossom—the first tree to do so, in February. It spoke to him of the wakening of nature; it was the "wake-up" tree, and he thought of Yahweh's watchfulness and wakefulness over His people (Jer. i, 11, 12). Read the verses in the Bible and then compare them with this translation: "The word of Yahweh came unto me, saying, 'Jeremiah, what seest thou?' And I said, 'I see a branch of a Wake-up tree.' Then said Yahweh unto me, 'Thou hast well seen; for I am wakeful over My word to perform it.'" Little did Jeremiah know what a hard task lay before him, how obstinate and stubborn would be his hearers, how persecuted, lonely and miserable he himself would be.

Jeremiah's Background

In order to understand his preachings and words we need to see how keenly he saw and remembered his home life. He had watched the migrating birds (viii, 7) and thought of their

Jeremiah's "wake-up" tree—almond blossom. Why is this a good description of the tree? What other tree can you see?

This jackal looks harmless, but Jeremiah knew well of its danger and habits.

wonderful homing instinct; he knew of the ways of the partridge (xvii, 11). In the wilderness he had known the dangers of wild animals (iv, 7; v, 6); there were bears, lions (no longer found in Palestine), leopards, hyenas, jackals and wild boars. Leaving the wilderness, Jeremiah had sometimes entered the depths of the Jordan gorge —the "pride of the Jordan". When he spoke of the invasion of the Babylonians he said, "Behold, he shall come like a lion from the pride of Jordan" (xlix, 19). And again (in xii, 5) he asked, "In a land of peace (safety) how wilt thou do in the pride of Jordan (danger)?" Like Hosea, he had seen the leopard with its yellow spots ringed with black, high in the craggy rocks waiting for sunset; he had known of its stealthy descent, its hunting for prey, and the deathly silence that reigned when it was on the prowl. For three nights it would wait motionless until an unsuspecting villager or sheep or even wild beast was near enough for its swift, deadly leap. So Jeremiah speaks of distrust—"Does an Ethiopian change his skin, or a leopard his spots?" (xiii, 23) —and of the danger of the watching, waiting enemy—"a leopard shall watch over their cities" (v, 6).

His Message for the Individual

For all this knowledge of the countryside, Jeremiah was evidently born into a priestly family, amongst the priests of Levi and a descendant of Eli (see Book I). He therefore knew much of the early writings and stories of his people, and may even have read some of the accounts of the Northern Kingdom that were brought to Judah when the scribes of Israel had fled before the conquering hordes of Assyria in 721 B.C. Like Amos and Isaiah he knew only too well how unfit and weak he was, but felt sure that

Yahweh would always help him in his bitter duty of challenging his own people (xv, 15–18; xxiii, 18, 22).

His message was straightforward but startling. If Judah continued to disobey Yahweh, the people would be punished—they had heard that from the other prophets. But Jeremiah had different ideas. He said that they would be punished both as a nation and also as individuals. This was a new teaching, the responsibility of the individual. The people had been used to the idea of being represented by a great leader—like Moses, for example—who could speak with God for the nation; but Jeremiah was now saying that Yahweh was concerned with each and every one of them separately, and looked for a change of heart in each individual, not merely in the nation or their leader (xxxi, 30–32).

There was a proverb in Israel: "The fathers have eaten sour grapes and the children's teeth are set on edge" (xxxi, 29: compare Ezek. xviii, 2, 3). Other prophets had said Yahweh would bring disaster upon the Jews because of their wicked history; but the people now said this was not fair, they ought not to be punished for their fathers' sins. Jeremiah told them that they themselves were wicked enough to deserve the punishment that was expected. Each one of them must

Both Hosea and Jeremiah knew the leopard, too. Assyria was described as stealthy as this animal (Hos. xiii, 7; Jer. v, 6).

Into a brazier of this kind Jehoiakim threw the pieces of skin bearing the prophecies of Jeremiah.

be judged for his own sins and wrong-doings. Josiah had tried to make them good with his reforms, but his work had been "from the outside". What was needed was something "inside" —a change of heart. This is often spoken of as Jeremiah's New Covenant—and new it certainly was in the ears of the Jews.

Forbidden to Preach

Knowing from their past history how easily the nation switched from evil to good and back again to evil, Jeremiah decided that only exile—as had happened to Israel—would teach them that Yahweh meant what He said (xxvii 1, 2, 7–11). He proclaimed this in no less a place than the Temple courts and was promptly seized by his enemies (vii, 1–16; xxvi, 1–16: compare Luke xix, 46). The Temple priests rescued him; there may have been some of his relations amongst them. They felt sure that his message was from Yahweh, but they forbade him ever again to preach in the precincts of the Temple. So he dictated his message to a young friend who became his secretary; this was Baruch, who took Jeremiah's words to the Temple and read them for all to hear. The prophet was hurried away to a place of safety, but the king—Jehoiakim—had the message read to him. It was the ninth month, November, and the winter had set in. The king therefore sat by a brazier, a fire of charcoal (not coal as we know it) burning in a copper pan mounted on a stand sixty centimetres high. The charcoal was probably from the root of broom (Ps. cxx, 4 and Job xxx, 4); sweet-smelling chips of pine might have been added to give the smoke a pleasant tang. The king listened to Jeremiah's prophecy of exile, and as he did so, with his knife he deliberately slashed pieces from the scroll and

watched them shrivel in the "coals of fire" (xxxvi, 22, 23). He sent for Jeremiah and Baruch, but they were safely away, ready to start all over again the message that the king had destroyed but which the prophet knew he must tell to the king's people (xxxvi, 28, 32).

It was at this time that a lesser prophet named Uriah had prophesied against the king, had fled to Egypt and was brought back to Jehoiakim, who had him murdered. Letters about this man, written on pieces of pottery called "ostraca", have been found at Lachish; they tell of the arrest and trial of Uriah and give interesting information about the people of the time. Jeremiah was more fortunate than Uriah, though he must have despaired of ever getting the people to listen to him.

A King of Assyria

Meanwhile, if Judah's lesson could be learned only through captivity, which nation would be her conquerer ? Assyria, weakened by her battles with Egypt and the Scythian hordes, had long since fallen. Ashurbanipal had become king— the most powerful of them all—but even he could not hold together the whole empire. Besides, he was a scholar rather than a fighter; he had an enormous library of clay tablets and cylinders in

Pieces of pottery like this are called "ostraca". On such a piece might be written notes, receipts, letters, etc., instead of on papyrus or skin. This one reads: "For the King, a thousand and one hundred (measures?) of oil (from?) Hiyahu", probably an Israelite customs officer!

Ashurbanipal and his Queen are feasting in their garden. Examine closely the throne, the divan, the slaves and the musicians.

cuneiform script—histories, stories, lists of plants, mathematics, chemicals, prescriptions (one of these recommends liquorice-root crushed in beer as a cure for coughing!). There were dictionaries, too, and translations of old Babylonian stories, including their legend of the Creation. Perhaps the king became too much interested in his learning or spent too much time feasting with his queen; his kingdom dwindled and it was soon after his death that Nineveh was destroyed by the Babylonians, now more correctly called the Chaldeans.

Judah in Danger

Babylon also subdued Egypt once more; Nebuchadrezzar now looked at Judah, a pearl by the wayside of the trade and war routes between Babylonia and Egypt. History repeats itself over and over again. Jeremiah saw in Babylonia the nation into whose hands Judah would fall. Yahweh's will was that Judah should be a god-fearing nation rather than a mighty one; and if the people went on worshipping baals, oppressing the poor, ignoring true worship, then they must be carried away from their land and in the loneliness of exile be sorry for their wickedness and prepare to return to Him. Bravely, Jeremiah came out of hiding. He went to the home of a potter and saw a message in the potter's work.

The potter was a familiar craftsman. He had his store of clay, a simple kiln or clay oven, and a rough shelter, even a rocky cave, for his booth. Having kneaded the clay to a soft consistency,

he placed it on a small wheel connected to a larger one beneath it by a strip of strong leather or a post. With his feet he turned the bottom wheel, which revolved the small one, and as it began to spin so he shaped his jars and pots and water vessels. If the jar broke or a flaw appeared in the making and it was spoiled, he stopped the wheel, took off the imperfect jar and remoulded the clay in order to begin again. From the imperfect he would make the perfect article. This, said Jeremiah, was what Yahweh would do to His people. They were like clay in His hands; they had become imperfect and He must now take them and reshape them to the vessel He wanted them to be; He would remould them to His purpose (Jer. xviii, 1–12).

In the Valley of the Son of Hinnom, at Potsherd Gate, the scene of child-sacrifice in the cruel reign of Manasseh, Jeremiah gathered the people around him and held aloft a potter's vessel; this was a narrow-necked drinking-vessel like the one shown in the picture of the water-carrier on p. 56.

Jeremiah proclaimed the words of Yahweh—that because of their sins and refusal to listen to His prophets, Jerusalem would be made desolate and the people would be given over to their enemies. Yahweh would break them as Jeremiah would break the potter's vessel, into so many pieces that "it cannot be made whole again". Whereupon the prophet dashed it to the ground, where it broke into smithereens. There was not left a sherd of any size for use in the house or by the well or for writing upon, and for the most part it lay fit only for grinding into powder and dust. This, said Jeremiah, was what Yahweh would do to His rebellious people—"dash them in pieces like a potter's vessel" (Ps. ii, 9; Isa. xxx, 14; Jer. xix).

Jerusalem Surrenders

Jeremiah's enemies were furious and put him in stocks at the mercy of those who jeered and sneered at him and pelted him with citrons and pomegranates. Meanwhile the king tried to "buy off" Nebuchadrezzar by paying tribute; he could not continue this, so he allied himself with Egypt and refused to pay any more. Nebuchadrezzar laid siege to Jerusalem in 597 B.C. The city surrendered; the king, his court, the principal leaders, craftsmen and smiths were taken to Babylon. Amongst these was Ezekiel, who was taken to Tel-abib on the River Chebar, near Babylon. Jeremiah's prophecies were beginning to come true. Ps. xlii and xliii tell how the people were banished from Judah and so from their own God. Jeremiah described this captivity in his parable of the baskets of figs; the good figs were those who had been carried off—they would learn their lesson and return to Judah determined to become servants of the true God; the future of Judah was in their hands. Those left behind were the bad figs (xxiv, 1–10); they would merely be cast away as useless.

Exile

The captives were not treated cruelly as had been those of the Northern Kingdom taken by Assyria; they were able to live amongst their captors, to work, to trade and even to rule. Yahweh did not wish them to be utterly destroyed as were the ten lost tribes. They were encouraged by a letter from Jeremiah, who advised them to settle down and accept their foreign yoke. Yahweh would be with them. This was difficult for some to accept, but through Jeremiah Yahweh had said, "Ye shall seek Me and find Me when ye search for Me with your whole heart ... and I will turn again your captivity" (xxix, 1–18).

The Prophet's Own Faith

Jeremiah was so certain of the return that he bought a piece of land in his own village—a risky chance, seeing that it was occupied by the enemy; he paid seven shekels and ten pieces of silver. At the time of the transaction he was in prison! In the Court of the Guard the deeds were drawn up; two copies were placed in an earthenware jar for preservation and given to Baruch for safekeeping (xxxii, 11).

The new king, Zedekiah, was changeable and weak-willed, eager to accept guidance from false prophets but equally sure he ought to listen to Jeremiah. Having angered Nebuchadrezzar by joining Egypt in yet another rebellion, he secretly

Another potter with a different method of working his feet. Jeremiah used this craftsman and his work to illustrate his warnings.

The water-carrier has filled the drinking vessel for a thirsty buyer who pours the water into his mouth without touching the spout with his lips. Why does he do this? The vessel is called a "bakbook" because that is the gurgling sound the water makes as it comes out.

sent for Jeremiah. Under the siege there was little food available, but the king gave him bread in the Street of Bakers, a short street in which the booths were all of the same trade.

Jerusalem Falls

But Zedekiah was strangely indecisive and even gave way to Jeremiah's enemies to the extent of letting them throw the prophet into a pit, waterless and slimy, from which he was rescued by a kindly Ethiopian court official; the king then promised Jeremiah safety if he would guide him in his difficult position. Jeremiah wore a yoke like that used over the necks of oxen when ploughing. "Bring your neck under the yoke of the king of Babylon; serve him and live," was his answer (xxxviii, 1–13). But Zedekiah, again accepting the advice of false prophets, revolted. Nebuchadrezzar moved southwards a second time, destroyed Lachish which the king had rebuilt, then laid siege to Jerusalem, as Jeremiah had said would happen. With their enormous siege-engines and skilled fighters the Babylonians swiftly captured the city, razed the Temple and palace to the ground. Zedekiah had to watch his sons and courtiers killed; then his own eyes were put out, and, chained, blinded and de-

feated, he was sent to Babylon. This was in 586 B.C.

Jeremiah's Choice

Jeremiah was set free and given his choice—safety and comfort in Babylon or hardship and disappointment in Judah. He decided to stay where he felt he could do most good, amongst his own folk; the "good figs" could look after themselves. Once more the strong and useful Jews were taken away, beyond the Euphrates; those left were poor, inefficient, old and lazy; it would be as much as they could manage to till the soil and tend the vineyards (xxxix, 1–xl, 6).

At last Judah was in captivity, as Jeremiah had prophesied, and—as we should say—"for her own good". See how Ps. lxxiv fits in here.

Meanwhile the prophet worked with the Babylonian governor Gedaliah, a Jew put in charge by Nebuchadrezzar. Many of the Jews who had fled from the invasion into the hills now returned, and then rebelled. They killed the governor and forced Jeremiah to go with them to Egypt, where they went to escape the revenge of the King of Babylonia, and where they hoped to find help and protection (xl, 1–5; xlii, 2–10, 19–22; xliii, 1–7; xliv, 29, 30).

Did Jeremiah finally escape to Babylon, or was he stoned to death in Egypt? We do not know. We do not know how far he succeeded in his difficult task, but we know with what courage he faced it. He was rejected, laughed at, hunted, thrown into prison, put into the stocks, dropped into a well, taken by force to a foreign land. Read what Paul says of his own experiences whilst serving God as a missionary and a preacher (2 Cor. xi, 23–27).

EXPRESSION WORK

1. What lessons does Jeremiah draw from his knowledge of the leopard and its ways?
2. What was Jeremiah's "New Covenant" (xxxi, 31–34)? Why is this part of his preaching so important?
3. Write for acting a dialogue between Jeremiah and Baruch.
   or
   Draw a "potter's vessel".
   or
   Act a dialogue between the water-carrier and the thirsty man, in the picture.

4. "Zedekiah was weak and indecisive." What does this mean and was it true?
5. List in parallel columns the experiences of Jeremiah and Paul.
6. Do you think Jeremiah should have gone to Babylon or was he right to stay in Jerusalem? Discuss this.
7. Compare and contrast the characters of Isaiah and Jeremiah.
8. In what ways are the life and work of Jeremiah "a message for the timid"? Use i, 7, 8; xi, 18–23; xv, 10–18; xx, 7–18, and other references telling of his experiences.
9. Letter and learn Phil. iv, 13. What has this to do with Jeremiah and his work?
10. Write in modern language Jeremiah's message to the Exiles (xxix, 10–14).
11. Act or draw Jeremiah in the stocks surrounded by scornful priests and jeering onlookers.
12. Prepare an Order of Service on Jeremiah, for Morning Assembly. You will need a theme or title, a suitable hymn, a reading and prayers; an extract from a modern writer might help too.

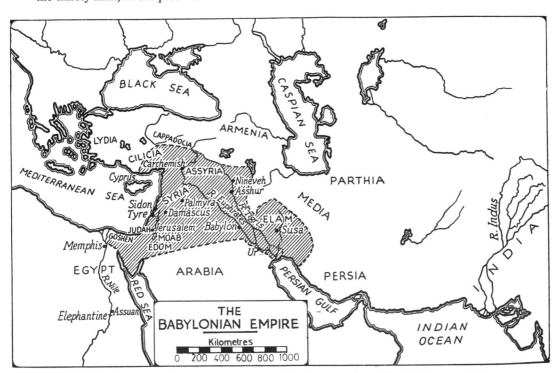

The extent of the Babylonian Empire. Compare it with the empires of Persia, Greece and Rome.

CHAPTER 9

THE EXILE:
EZEKIEL AND SECOND ISAIAH

(Ezekiel i, 1–3, 7, 8, 11; ii. 1–7; iii, 10–13; vi, 8; xviii; xx, 12, 13; xxxiv, 11–16; xxxvi;
xxxvii, 1–14; xliv, 24. Isaiah xl, 1–31; xlii, 1–15; xli, 5–39; xliii; xliv, 9–28; xlv; xlix, 1–16;
l, 4–9; lii, 1–15; liii. Ezra i, Psalm cxxvi; cxxxvii)

The Jewish Dispersion

FOR the next fifty years (586–539 B.C.) the history of the Jews is a blank; the national life of Judah seemed to be extinct; its peoples were scattered far and wide through the then known world. This is known as the Jewish Dispersion. As we examine the movements more closely we can see three main groups. There is one settlement in Babylon; this consisted of the more wealthy and intelligent leaders and crafts-men taken captive after Nebuchadrezzar's first siege of Jerusalem. These Jews we shall consider later in this chapter, for they were being taught their lesson—in Babylon, as Jeremiah had said they must; they were preparing for the return, in Yahweh's own good time, to their home-land.

A second group was made up of the peasants and poorer people, the "bad figs" left behind after the second devastation of the city. They had no leaders, no craftsmen, no farmers; they allowed Judah to become a wilderness, for they were without hope, miserable and beaten; their Temple was gone and they believed that Yahweh had forsaken them.

The third group is not easy to see. It consisted of scattered communities and settlements. To one of these Jeremiah was taken against his will, in Egypt. Places like Assuan and Memphis had these groups; fugitives from home, they re-membered their God and built temples. Later events indicate that amongst them were soldiers and leaders, for papyrus records written in Aramaic, a Semitic dialect, and belonging to such a community, have been found at Elephan-tine in Upper Egypt. They seem to have wor-shipped Yahweh, but also served two other gods; the Egyptian priests appear to have interfered

A view of the Euphrates. The Exiles missed sadly their Judaean rugged countryside; they found this low, marshy land monotonous by comparison with the mountains, ravines and deserts of their own land.

One of the Gates of Babylon as it may have appeared to the Exiles. Studded with gold, with its raised carvings of animals, it was massive and imposing.

with their worship too. Other colonies were in Damascus (1 Kings xx, 34), in Persia, Rome and Pontus (Turkey) (Acts ii, 9–11).

Captive in Babylon

In Babylon, the first captives came quickly to the notice of the king and were allowed considerable freedom in their worship and ways of living; they took a share in education and commerce, and before long their national unity began to reassert itself. If Judah was to recover, it must be through the exiles whose faith was being sorely tried. The elders and priests resumed their former rôles and took over the communities as they had done in Jerusalem. Others, like Nehemiah and Zerubbabel, did so well that they entered the king's court; some stayed when it was taken over by Persian rulers—as is shown by the stories of Daniel and his three friends.

The Wonders of Babylon

What did the exiles find in the city of Babylon? In 2 Kings xviii, 32, we are told that Babylon was a land of corn, wine, vineyards and olives, to the exiles "a land like their own land". Its fertility depended upon the two great rivers whose wide, flat valleys formed much of the Fertile Crescent, and as the Egyptians controlled the Nile waters for the fertility of Egypt, so the Babylonians had to harness the waters of the Euphrates, the "soul of the land", and the Tigris, "bestower of blessings"; a network of canals irrigated the country and the peasants worked

The city is long since devastated, its glory is gone. Here are excavated walls and a gateway as it now is.

One of the seven wonders of the world. An artist portrays the Hanging Gardens described on this page.

the shadufs and water-wheels to provide the water necessary for their crops. There was great heat and the air was clear; the nights must have been of great beauty, brilliantly lit with stars (Isa. xlvii, 13).

The buildings were for the most part of bricks made from clay and bound with natural bitumen or pitch found near the city. Larger buildings such as those of Nebuchadrezzar were built of stones brought from Mesopotamia. The king is known to have been a great builder, and the Jews, accustomed though they were to the magnificence of their own city, its Temple, palace and chief buildings, must have been amazed at the wonderful sights they now saw. The Hanging Gardens (one of the seven wonders of the world) reared high before them; over vaulted chambers or cells the gardens were built in tiers or terraces watered by shafts sunk deep into the Euphrates. Here, too, were the great temple of Merodach (Marduk), "Lord of Heaven and Earth", flanked by winged figures, and the enormous Tower of Babel or Ziggurat (see Gen. xi, 1–9 and Book I, Chapter 1). This was the "House of the Foundation of Heaven and Earth", of which Nebuchadrezzar wrote, "I raised the summit of the Tower of Stages so that its top rivalled the heavens."

When pinnacles toppled down, as they sometimes did, it was said that the gods were very angry and must be appeased.

On New Year's Day, Marduk was taken out of his temple, put on a ship and drawn along red-stoned Babel Street into white-paved Procession Street, and through the huge gold-covered city gates, for worship at a special shrine. The king in his royal robes attended and the crowds—including open-mouthed, awe-struck Jews—thronged the Ishtar Gate or climbed the walls to watch. And such walls they were—two hundred cubits high, fifty wide, moated all round. Houses lined the top, with room for four horse-chariots to turn; over a hundred gates, fronted with solid brass, gave access to the city. Such massive strength seemed impregnable, yet Cyrus of Persia entered easily and Alexander of Greece died in one of its brilliantly adorned palaces two hundred years after that.

Keeping Faith with God

Psalm cxxxvii makes it clear that many of the Jews in Babylon now felt that Yahweh had forsaken them as they had forsaken Him. These turned to their conquerors' gods, which now seemed so much more powerful than Yahweh

An old Judaean, typical of those in Exile. "How shall we sing the Lord's song in a strange land?" Ps. cxxxvii, 4.

—and wrote down those that had been handed on hitherto by word of mouth; these scribes, as they were called, tended to alter as they wrote, often to please themselves or to give reasons for events and happenings. (You will remember how Gehazi's leprosy was given a "reason".) They revised the Books of the Law, especially Deuteronomy—found in the reign of Josiah, you will recall—and the histories of Joshua, the Judges and Kings. They were determined that the nation's life and faith should not die. The records called P documents were written in Hebrew, which was the language of the Canaanites amongst whom the Jews had settled when they first entered Palestine, under Joshua. This tongue was retained whilst the Jews were in captivity, but later, under the influence of Greece—after the conquests of Alexander the Great—the upper classes spoke Greek and Latin, and Hebrew dropped out of use except in the synagogue and Temple worship. The ordinary folk also developed amongst themselves during this time the dialect called Aramaic. Some of the Book of Ezra is in this language. If you look closely at the Hebrew writing given on p. 63 you will notice the strange shapes of the symbols. They are all consonants; the dots and dashes represent the

and worship of which was so much more splendid and realistic. But some remembered what Jeremiah had said, and his message assured them of Yahweh's presence with them even in a foreign land. It was these who met and devised plans whereby their Jewish home and religious life should be maintained. They began to prepare for their eventual return to Judah; this meant detailed lists of names and families; rules and customs, rites and ceremonies—especially of Temple worship—were drawn up. They found that one day each week was already kept by their captors as a kind of day of rest or sabbath; this enabled the Jews to keep the same day for attending to their own worship, to talk over the scriptures and prophecies which they now read more frequently. These meetings were the beginnings of synagogue worship that was to be the accepted form of Jewish worship down to the present day.

Preserving the Scriptures

During this period, too, priests and scribes interested in the stories and histories of their ancient land compiled and revised these records—the J and E documents referred to in Chapter 5

They remembered their city, as all Jews have done—"If I forget thee, O Jerusalem . . ." Ps. cxxxvii, 5.

The Exiles recalled the narrow street in which they lived. Even today it is narrow, supported with arches, with lattice windows.

the people of what might happen to them. In xxxiii, 21, the fall of the city is announced; then the book continues with messages of hope and thoughts of the return. Ezekiel says much of what Amos and Isaiah had already said; he sees the danger of Babylonian idol-worship. He condemns and warns the exiles that it is no use their excusing themselves or blaming their forefathers. Like Jeremiah he was unpopular, but he brought hope to those who believed that because Yahweh was interested in them as individuals they could worship Him wherever they were—even in Babylonia. In this way Ezekiel helped to preserve the Jewish religion and he had much to do with the rites and ceremonial aspects of the sanctuary, priesthood and laws (see Ezek. xxxvi, 35).

In chapters i and ii Ezekiel describes his call and vividly portrays his wonderful vision, trying to explain his thoughts of Yahweh's majesty, power, strength and speed through pictures of the winged faces of a lion, a man, an ox and an eagle. This call came six years before Jerusalem fell, and for those six years he seemed to have worked in vain.

vowels. The original word we know as YAHWEH was YHWH; the vowels are from another Hebrew word for LORD, and when this occurs in the Bible in capital letters it should be read as YAHWEH. But when the scribes wrote the scriptures during their exile, they wrote only in consonants; the vowels were a later addition to make the accounts more easy to read and to understand.

Two men felt they must do a great deal for their fellow-men whilst they were in Babylon. One was Ezekiel, before and during the exile itself; the other was Second Isaiah, at the time the Persians were about to take over the Babylonian (Chaldean) Empire.

EZEKIEL

Ezekiel certainly knew Jeremiah well; he may have been one of the friendly priests who rescued Jeremiah from the Temple and was probably amongst the first Jews to be taken into captivity. His writings are difficult to understand. The early part of his book contains the messages he preached before the fall of Jerusalem, warning

His Message

In the second part of his book he describes in pictures the restoration and return of the Jews. Chapter xxxiv tells of the good shepherd, a figure familiar to the exiles; compare it with the account given in Matt. xviii, 12–14 and Luke xix, 10. In chapter xxxvi he tells of the ruin of Moab, Edom and other nations who had closed in on the defenceless Judah that the exiles had left behind; he goes on to tell of the return to their simple agricultural life in Judah. This, says Ezekiel, will prove to idol-worshipping nations that Yahweh, the God of Judah, is a strong God. An even more striking picture is found in chapter xxxvii, where Ezekiel describes his vision of the Valley of Dry Bones. It was not unusual to pass on a journey the remains of armies or the dead of caravans that had been attacked, and the Jews had seen their bones whitening in the hot sun. Ezekiel uses this memory to make it clear to the Jews that the nation, now dead in exile, is to be given new life: "I will bring you into the land of Israel and ye shall live." This seemed impossible at the time to everyone except Ezekiel. The prophet adds a symbol of unity; the two sticks stand for the two kingdoms of Judah and Ephraim (Israel); they are now seen as one nation with a covenant of peace between them and with Yahweh's sanctuary "in the midst of them for evermore".

The new covenant is to be a new stage in their history, for Yahweh would return to His Temple and to them; they would be a holy people in a holy city under the care of a Holy God. It is in this thought that Ezekiel echoes the teaching of Isaiah that the "remnant of Israel" would be a holy people; he also strengthens the teaching of Jeremiah, who had taught the responsibility of the individual. Ezekiel says that individuals must worship *together* for the full spiritual benefit of each person. This is nowadays an accepted belief, that individuals best serve in a community—whether it be a church or a school or other group of people with the same ideals of life.

Before any of the exiles returned to Judah, the priest-prophet died, but his influence continued throughout the years to come; for not only did he establish a formal type of worship, but he also kept together the small number of Jews who were really anxious to return, when the time came, to begin their nation anew.

SECOND ISAIAH

The really great prophet of this period is Second Isaiah, living from about 550 B.C. We do not know his name. His writings are in the Book of Isaiah, chapters xl–lv; he is called Second Isaiah (in some books, Deutero-Isaiah) to distinguish him from the Isaiah of the first chapters of the Book and of whom we have already read in Chapters 6 and 7 of this book. His writings are at least two hundred years later than those of the first Isaiah. He speaks to the exiles of hope and deliverance. Most of the original exiles were by then dead, and their children and grandchildren knew of Jerusalem only by name and story. They were now prosperous and did not particularly want to return to this city of their fathers, where it might be difficult, even dangerous, to live; it was far distant, too, and to reach it they would have to make a hazardous journey. In any case, it seemed foolish to return to this place when Yahweh could equally well be worshipped in Babylonia. Jeremiah had said so, and they would accept his word (xxix, 5–7); and many of them certainly had proved the truth of this in their own lives.

His Message

Second Isaiah makes it clear that Cyrus is to deliver the Jews by conquering Babylonia; he is the "Lord's anointed" and "My shepherd" (xliv, 28; xlv). Isaiah reasserts the teachings of the earlier prophets, that Yahweh is Creator, that He loves, that He may be worshipped anywhere, that to worship Him is a personal matter.

The exiles had suffered but had learned to trust Him; for the second time in their history they were to move into the Promised Land, and they and their scattered kinsmen were to be

The Hebrew language. The signs are consonants and the dots are vowels (see p. 61). The large words mean "Repentance, Prayer, Charity". The reading is from right to left.

united and restored to their homes. Even the Gentiles (people of other nations) would see and acknowledge Yahweh's power (xlix, 6 and xlii, 6); and they would accept Him as Lord God. This duty—the revealing of God to the Gentiles—was one that the Jews were reluctant to carry out. These are familiar chapters, read and sung in our schools and churches throughout the year. They all speak joyously, even exuberantly, of the exiles' future—provided the people gave up their idol-worship and wickedness.

The Foolishness of Idol-worship

In chapter xliv, 9–20, Second Isaiah writes an almost amusing jibe at idolatry. There were many idols in Babylon, many gods, too—Marduk, Shamash, Bel, Nebo, small ones, great ones, gods in gold, bronze, stone and wood; it was easy to worship these figures that could be seen and difficult to worship Yahweh Who could not be seen. Second Isaiah says: Look at this idol; watch the craftsman making it; he chooses the tree, cuts it down, shapes the figure, burns the wood chips and shavings, carries it around and stands it up—and then, bowing down before it, expects it to help him! How stupid this is, says the prophet. "Deliver me," says the man, "for thou art my god." Read xlvi, 6, 7 and Psalm cxv, 4–8. There can be no other God but Yahweh, says Second Isaiah. Now, choose. Leave your comfort, your money, your position; return to the flock of righteousness and peace, with Yahweh as the Great Shepherd, for you are His chosen flock, His people. Both Ezekiel (xxxiv) and Isaiah (xl, 11) use the familiar idea of the shepherd, as Jesus was to do many years later.

The "Servant Songs"

Second Isaiah is certain that God's purpose will be fulfilled (lv, 8 ff.), and he writes some wonderful poems which are now called the Servant Songs. These are found in xlii, 1–7—his call; xlix, 1–6—his failure, l, 4–9—his trust; lii, 13–53 —his faithfulness. Some scholars say that the prophet was thinking of Jesus and His Crucifixion; he probably was not, but Jesus in His service and suffering could well be described by these verses; He could easily be the Servant.

EXPRESSION WORK

1. What was the Jewish Dispersion?
2. Pretend you are exiles watching celebrations on New Year's Day in Babylon. Describe what you see.
3. Draw the Hanging Gardens, *or* construct them from matchboxes or balsa wood or cardboard.
4. How was synagogue-worship begun?
5. Write in your own words the Vision of the Valley of Dry Bones. What does it mean?
6. You are an Israelite slave who has escaped from Assyria. Talk about your experiences to an exile in Babylon.
7. Ezekiel pictures a kind of "New Jerusalem". See also Zech. viii, 4, 5. Find Blake's poem *Jerusalem*. What have these writers in common?
8. What was the message of Second Isaiah? How did his thoughts of God differ from Ezekiel's?
9. Let Isaiah reason with a craftsman on the foolishness of idol-worship (xlvi).
10. Relate in your own words the parables of Ezekiel found in Ezek. xvii, 1–10 and xix, 1–9. Give your own titles.
11. What are the Servant Songs? How can they be related to Jesus?
12. (*a*) Learn Isa. xl, 1–11 and 28–31.
    (*b*) Prepare for Choral Speaking in Morning Assembly Psalm cxxxvii.

A shofar (ram's horn), carved with sacred Hebrew writings. It is blown by the priest as a call to prayer. See Gen. xxii and Lev. xxiii, 26-32.

CHAPTER 10

THE RETURN:
HAGGAI AND ZECHARIAH,
NEHEMIAH AND EZRA

(Haggai ii, 1–9. Ezra i, 1–11; viii, 21–36; x, 7–10. Zech. ii, 1–6; vii, 8–14. Neh. i; ii; iii;
iv; vi; viii, 1–8)

Cyrus

BABYLON had lost her great king Nebuchad-rezzar in 562 B.C., and despite various campaigns in Edom and Syria, her last king had begun to feel the pressure from Media; then, almost without warning, about 550 B.C., an unknown king of Persia appeared on the scene and became king of the western empires of Media and Persia, obviously set upon extending his con-

quests even further. Second Isaiah spoke of him as the deliverer of the exiles; there are references, too, in Psalm cxxxvii, 1–6 and Ezek. i, 1–3. Egypt, Lydia and Sparta joined Babylon in an attempt to stop Cyrus, but Croesus of Lydia (known to us for his great wealth and first use of coins for money) was defeated and Cyrus was master of a growing empire that was to last for two hundred and fifty years. Look at your maps and see how

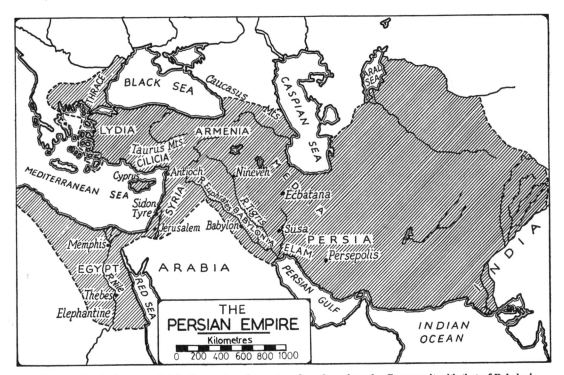

The Persian Empire has extended further eastwards, westwards and northwards. Compare it with that of Babylonia.

The cylinder seal of Darius, King of Persia. It shows the king in his chariot, hunting lions. The flying figure is Mazda (Ormuzd), the sun-god, protector of the king.

he advanced through these nations—Babylon, Western Arabia, Mesopotamia, Asia Minor. The maps of the Assyrian and Babylonian Empires are on the same scale and should be compared closely with the map of the Persian Empire.

Persian Rule

Having taken control of the irrigation system of canals on which life in the city depended, Cyrus marched into Babylon in 538 B.C. This is recorded on a broken cylinder of baked clay called Cyrus' Cylinder, now kept in the British Museum; Cyrus says that the conquest was "without battle and without fighting", but see Jer. xxv, 12; li. Cyrus introduced a new idea of rule over conquered nations, probably because as a boy he had learned much about justice and honour. He learned, too, "to ride, to use the bow, and to speak the truth". Although he was a dictator, he was a noble one and a fine statesman. On his tomb are written these words: "I am Cyrus, who won the empire for the Persians. Grudge me not therefore this handful of earth which covers me."

The Assyrians had believed in complete extermination of the nations they defeated; the Babylonians took their best captives to their own land and allowed them to continue their own way of life; but the Persians did not believe in either oppression or captivity; they wanted the nations they ruled to be happy and content, realising they would accept conquest the more easily. Cyrus set up local governors and rulers of their own race, encouraged their religion and made it easy for them, if they were already captives in a foreign land, to return if they wished to their homeland.

Judah

For the Jews this meant that they could continue their own religion and mode of worship and think about their return "home" with even greater freedom. Cyrus knew that Judah needed attention. During the fifty years of the exile it had been ravaged and invaded by surrounding nations and had become a wilderness (Hag. i, 5, 6, 10, 11; ii, 15–19). Even the language had changed and instead of Hebrew the Jews were speaking a Syrian dialect called Aramaic; Jesus spoke this tongue nearly six hundred years later (see 2 Kings xviii, 28; Mark v, 41 and vii, 34). Jerusalem had been levelled to the ground; armies had swept through the land where the people had tried miserably to build and rebuild their poor homes with débris from the ruined cities and villages. In the south Edom had advanced, to the north was Tyre, to the west Philistia, to the east Moab; they were closing in —and who could save her?

The Return

It was with high hopes that some of the descendants of the exiles at last prepared to return to Jerusalem, in the first year of Cyrus, King of Persia, in 536 B.C. Won over by Second Isaiah's enthusiasm and encouragement, they looked forward with great joy to the task and duty of rebuilding their fathers' city. For their further help, Cyrus allowed Sheshbazzar, a prince of Judah, to lead the returning Judaeans; he gave them gold, silver, cattle, horses, mules, asses, camels and even the Temple vessels that Nebuchadrezzar had taken from Jerusalem for the House of Merodach—for it was the Temple of Yahweh that they were planning to build; houses and homes could come later. We are told that 42,000 people journeyed in that great caravan, but this is probably an exaggeration. Many of the Jews stayed in Babylon, perhaps to await news of the first return, and very likely because of their prosperity which they wanted to keep; but they later sent money to help the work that was being done in Jerusalem. It is not clear which way the caravan went; probably northwards through the Fertile Crescent, by Nineveh, Haran, with its ziggurat outlined against the sky, Carchemish, where Pharaoh Necho had been defeated by the Babylonians, across the Euphrates, and then southwards along the "Royal Road" as Abraham had done so many years before them. They were very anxious to see for themselves the Jerusalem about which they had heard so much.

Disappointment

But in Judah they found desolation and destruction, famine and wasteland. The "bad figs" were antagonistic, there was jealousy and fear—which was not surprising after all those years. New religious centres had been set up at Mizpah, Jericho and Bethel, for Jerusalem was in ruins and it had seemed pointless to build another centre of worship in a devastated city. However, the returned exiles began to rebuild the Temple, but they had no real heart in the work; the people of Jerusalem watched them, refused to help and even hindered them, and during the next sixteen years very little was done. Their disappointment crushed them; they had hoped for so much when they were in exile, but here there was only bitterness and opposition and failure.

Darius Rules

The Persian Empire tottered somewhat on the death of Cyrus, but when Darius took over from Cambyses, who had added Egypt to the empire,

he strengthened his control by dividing the whole empire into twenty-eight "satrapies" or provinces, each under a satrap or civil governor who was responsible for law and order, raising taxes and collecting tribute. Each governor was placed in a principal city, and was watched by officials called the "Eyes and Ears of the Great King". Only Darius could make a decision, and once it was made it was final—the "law of the Medes and Persians". He kept in touch with his satraps by means of couriers, whose horses were stabled along the many roads he had built to link up his provinces. His capital cities were at Persepolis, Babylon, Susa and Ecbatana; he also issued his own gold coins bearing his image and called "darics" (Ezra ii, 69; Neh. vii, 70). Tribute from conquered nations kept him in luxury; we know that from Arabia came frankincense, from Ethiopia gold, ebony, ivory—and every five years, five children!

Egypt again rebelled and Darius subdued her; then he marched into Asia Minor, conquered Scythia to the north of the Black Sea, and continued westwards until he was checked at

A Persian water-wheel, probably little changed from those seen by the Exiles under their Persian conquerors. How does it work?

Marathon. (This is probably a familiar word to some of you.)

Darius also encouraged the Jews in their building of the Temple. Having found the decree of Cyrus, he gave further gifts of all kinds (Ezra vi, 1–5; v, 8).

HAGGAI AND ZECHARIAH

At this time a new prophet arose—Haggai. He was a very practical man, anxious to get things done. In 520 B.C. he preached in favour of rebuilding the Temple. With the help of Darius, a second caravan of exiles had come to Judah under Zerubbabel the governor, a prince in the line of David. Read Esdras iii and iv (in the Apocrypha) and find how Zerubbabel obtained permission to come to Jerusalem. With Zechariah, Haggai declared that it was wrong of the people to build "panelled houses" for their own comfort and that the Temple must be built first; then the country would blossom plentifully once more —but not until. We find that on the site of the destroyed altar of Solomon's Temple a new one had been erected on their arrival in 536 B.C. The Feast of Tabernacles was then celebrated (see Book I). To remind them that the Children of Israel had once lived in tents in the wilderness, the people set up little booths or shelters made of branches of trees in the open air and lived in them; they offered their sacrifices on the new altar. Cedar trees from Lebanon were again

floated from Tyre to Joppa and brought by camels overland to Jerusalem; carpenters and masons and other craftsmen began to put into practice the crafts they had learned from their fathers whilst in Babylon so as to be ready for the rebuilding, already delayed for sixteen years.

The Samaritans

Haggai and Zechariah preached encouragement and worked hard; and at last the foundations of the Temple were laid. Meanwhile the worshippers at Bethel offered to help. These were the descendants of the Israelites who had intermarried with the people of other nations brought in by the Assyrians; they even worshipped Yahweh alongside the gods of those nations. Haggai spoke bluntly to them and said they were unclean; he refused their offer of help, so making them bitter enemies. These people were later called the Samaritans, and in their home at Shechem (now called Nablus) they never forgot the snub of Haggai. This explains the many jibes and bitter references to the Samaritans during our Lord's time, for the Jews "had no dealings" with them. They evidently built their own temple on Mt. Gerizim, and there is a Samaritan community there to this day (see picture on p. 72).

The "New Jerusalem"

Both Haggai and Zechariah hoped that Zerubbabel would restore the line of kingship and so

Over the Lebanon Mts. the returning Exiles saw shepherds with their sheep below the terraced foothills.

Here is a harvesting scene in Samaria—threshing, winnowing, sifting; and the scornful camel waits patiently.

fulfil the prophecies of Isaiah xi and Jer. xxiii, 5 and xxxiii, 15; but he disappears, probably recalled by a suspicious Darius. Zechariah's book is mainly one of visions, foretelling Yahweh's return to Jerusalem and the establishing of righteousness (viii, 16, 17). He looks forward to the time that the Temple would be the centre of the Jewish faith all over the world (ii, 10–13; viii, 20–23). His vision of the "New Jerusalem" (viii, 4, 5) is well known. Ezra records (vi, 15) that the Temple was finished in the sixth year of Darius, from which we date the dedication as being in 516 B.C. Passover was immediately celebrated (vi, 12, 20).

NEHEMIAH

Darius had tried and failed to conquer Greece, having been stopped at Marathon. His son Xerxes also tried and though defeating Leonidas at Thermopylae was himself checked at Salamis. Then came Artaxerxes; under him there was a second attempt by the exiles to return to Jerusalem. The story in Ezra is rather confused, but scholars tell us that Nehemiah, a Jew, came to Palestine before Ezra, in 445 B.C. From his brother he had heard how the exiles had been hindered in their building of the walls by raiders and tribes bearing down upon the unprotected city. As cupbearer to the king he was much in his master's company. His duty was to taste the wine before handing it to the king to drink—poisoning was not unknown in those days! He was also the king's friend; so, urged by the sad news he

constantly heard from merchants travelling from far-off Palestine into the markets of Babylon, he dared to plead that he might go to Jerusalem. He was a loyal Jew bound in exile, but longing to help in rebuilding the city. The king was sympathetic and gave him leave of absence and the official governorship of Jerusalem for a limited period; he also gave a grant of timber for rebuilding the walls.

Nehemiah at Work

Nehemiah found the Persian satraps Sanballat and Tobiah jealous of him; they stirred up strife. But in his capacity as governor Nehemiah was the equal of the two satraps and went about his work without fear, although he was well aware that they would even murder him in an effort to get rid of one of the king's "Eyes and Ears".

By night he examined the walls and planned how best to repair them. He divided the workers into groups, each to work upon a given section of the walls. Despite sneers and active hindrance —mainly from the satraps and the Samaritans— with half his men working and half watching (iv; vi, 1–14), Nehemiah saw his task completed in fifty-two days, "because the people had a mind to work". The walls were dedicated in a religious ceremony (xii, 30–40). The story is vividly told in his book; see also Ecclesiasticus xlix, 13.

Nehemiah found that there was oppression of the poor (v), not unlike that found and denounced by Amos hundreds of years before. Money-

Cedars of Lebanon, for centuries the wood of temples, palaces and ships.

lenders, in particular, were overcharging at high interest in their dishonest trading. He called the rich men together and made them promise not to force their claims on the poor who had lost their lands and property so soon after returning from exile. He set them a personal example by paying for the freedom of slaves and by not accepting taxes due to him from poor people who could not afford to pay. He then returned to Susa (see map), twelve years having elapsed since he had left his master.

His Second Visit

Artaxerxes gave him permission to return to the city as governor. When he did so, twelve years later, he found that his old enemies were strong and in powerful control. The sabbath was being desecrated, buying and selling were going on as if it were an ordinary day of the week. Nehemiah took swift action: he turned out the offenders neck and crop. Some were literally chased out, had their furniture thrown out of the city and their hair pulled! (See xiii, 25.) He made everybody pay charges and taxes for the upkeep of the Temple and insisted that there was to be no sabbath trading there or anywhere else. He made laws forbidding intermarriage with Ammonite and Moabite women, for the children of such marriages were speaking a foreign tongue and following foreign gods. The Book of Ruth (see Book I) was written to challenge such a policy as this, for it tells how Ruth, a Moabite,

married Boaz, a Judaean, and they became the great-grandparents of David, King of Israel. However, Nehemiah wanted to keep the race of Jews all of one blood and he felt that it was wrong for them to marry into other nations.

A group of seventy of the chief Jews promised Nehemiah to keep the Law and to see that others did also. These seventy became the Sanhedrin, of whom we hear more in the New Testament; their leader eventually became the High Priest, the most important person in Jerusalem.

"My Messenger"

We note here the Book of Malachi—about 400 B.C. The name is usually accepted as that of yet another prophet, but it is only a name meaning "My Messenger" given to a roll of scriptures, especially to iii, 1 and iv, 4–8. In this book foreign marriages are denounced; it challenges the Jews on their injustices (iii, 5) and on the careless way in which they follow the rules of worship. The writer also points out that some of them are so mean as to offer blind, lame and sick animals for sacrifice (i, 6–8); this was the very sin the Israelites had committed in the time of Amos. One wonders just how much the people had learned from these great prophets. Chapter iii, 1–3 contains some words familiar to those who know Handel's *Messiah*.

EZRA

Thirty-five years were to pass before yet another band of exiles returned, this time under

In Exile, the Jews met to read their precious scriptures; today, the Jews of the Dispersion still meet to do this in their synagogues all over the world.

Ezra, in 397 B.C. Ezra was a priest, ever anxious to teach the Law. Accepting the fact that the common tongue was now Aramaic, he made sure that the people understood the Law—the Pentateuch—by having it read in their own tongue. Some of his book is written in the language too.

When he had made clear to them what was expected of loyal Jews, he ordered the celebration of the Feast of Tabernacles and they solemnly promised to keep the Law. Some of his own company broke both Nehemiah's and his own rules against marrying non-Jewish women and caused Ezra great bitterness and anger. But, unlike Nehemiah, he merely pulled his own beard!

As a scribe, Ezra insisted upon restoring the rules and rites they had practised in exile and with which they were all familiar. Synagogues were set up in towns and villages; schools were begun so that the children might learn their Jewish history and religious faith. Wherever at least ten males could meet (women did not count!) and there was a copy of the Law, there they could have a synagogue. This gave rise to many synagogues throughout Palestine and in the surrounding countries where there were Jewish communities. It also made the scribes important, for it was their duty to write out the scriptures and to explain the details of the Law. By the time of Christ they held very high positions.

The Temple was made more beautiful, though the Ark was no longer there; we do not know what happened to it. Some say that Shishak took it when he invaded Judah under Rehoboam, soon after the division of Palestine; others say that Jeremiah hid it just before the destruction of Jerusalem and it was never found.

Even today the Jews "rejoice in the Law" and carry the Torah (the Law) round their synagogue as their forefathers did 2,500 years ago.

Here is the Samaritan Scroll—the Pentateuch. It is over 2,000 years old, written on the hair side of skins of sacred sheep and lambs. The roll is 18 m long, made up of 50 skins. It is kept at Nablus, the modern Shechem.

Prophecy Dies

So began the new community in Jerusalem. The outlook of the people was as narrow as their religion, but they fought bravely against all sorts of difficulties and dangers. Their loyalty was to Yahweh, Who became for them the God of Jerusalem rather than the God of Creation; which is probably why the Temple itself continued to be the centre of Jewish thought and life as well as of worship. A coldness of ritual had now come to their religion; and in the priestly atmosphere of what is known as Judaism, the fiery challenge of prophecy seemed to die. It was not to blaze again for four centuries, when the fierce words of John the Baptist proclaimed the old cry of the prophets—Repent!

EXPRESSION WORK

1. In what way was Cyrus the "deliverer" of the Exiles?
   or
   Pretend you are Cyrus and dictate the record of your victories to the scribe writing on your cylinder. Copy some of the cuneiform script used.
2. The god Mazda (Ormuzd) was the Persian god of pure light and fire; a holy man named Zoroaster preached about him in Persia in 600 B.C. Find out all you can about him and his religion, Zoroastrianism.
3. How did Aramaic become the common form of speech in place of Hebrew?
4. Trace on a map the route of the Return. Discuss, as travellers, your leave-taking, journey and arrival.
   or
   Write a diary to cover your journey from Babylon to Jerusalem.
5. Write and act a scene between Haggai and the chief Samaritan.
6. Use the following references and say what the men concerned had to say about the sabbath: Amos, viii, 5; Jer. xvii, 21–27; Ezek. xx, 13; xxii, 8; xxiii, 38; Neh. v, 1–19; xiii, 6.
7. Draw a Persian soldier. Draw also a section of the wall being built by Nehemiah's men.
8. Prepare a wall-frieze showing the Fall of Jerusalem, the Exile and the Return.
9. Write and act a scene between Nehemiah and his king.
   or
   Read Esdras iii, iv. Let Zerubbabel tell in his own words what led to his successful request to return to Jerusalem.
10. As Nehemiah, issue instructions to your men.
11. As a soldier, send a letter home, telling the family of your experiences whilst building the wall.
12. "Ezra probably saved the Jewish race from being absorbed as the Northern Tribes had been." Discuss this and try to decide at what cost this was probably true.

The Greeks under Alexander swept into Persia. Here, a Greek and a Persian soldier fight a duel to the death.

CHAPTER 11

THE GREEK EMPIRE
AND THE MACCABEES

(1 Macc. i, 1–9; ii, 1–48; iii, 1–iv, 61; 2 Macc. iv, 1–17; vi, 12–vii, 42)

FOR the next great influence on the history of the Jews we have to go to Greece and to trace briefly the rise and power of Alexander the Great. His father had begun to unite the Greek cities that for many years had existed as separate centres of rule, even fighting one another for control of the country; but he was murdered a short time after the first Olympic Games, in 336 B.C. Alexander's tutor was no less a person than Aristotle, a Greek philosopher and thinker whose teaching about kingship and government, learn-

ing, art and beauty had a lasting and deep influence upon Alexander, whose ambition was to conquer the world and spread these ideals by means of the Greek language, thought and culture.

Alexander's Conquests

He decided to begin with the Persian Empire. In Daniel vii, 6, Alexander is pictured as a winged leopard, swift and deadly. He won battle after battle. Through Asia Minor into Syria,

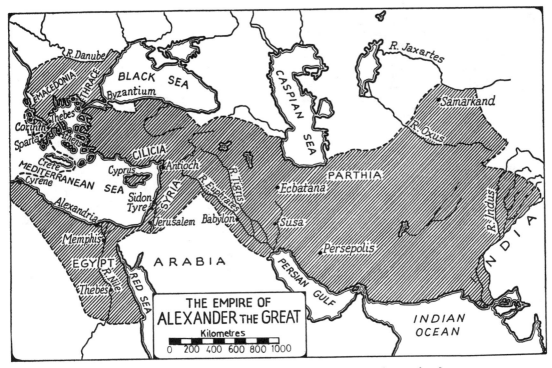

Alexander's Empire. Compare it with the other empires so far mentioned.

A statue of Alexander the Great in full armour—356–323 B.C.

This introduction of Greek customs and culture is called "hellenising" the cities and land. Every city had its public baths and gymnasium and theatre, its senate or political assembly for governing the people, its feasts and its philosophical discussions and arguments. Greek was the common tongue at least for trade and learning; it was easy to read and write. So began the Age of the Hellenes—the true name for the Greeks, used even today.

Alexander died in 323 B.C. at the age of thirty-two, in Babylon, having in thirteen years conquered the known world. But the result of his campaigns was the spread of Greek culture throughout the conquered nations as far as Rome.

The Gods of Greece

Many are the stories of heroes, poets, philosophers and orators, but we have no space to tell of them. Their gods and goddesses were known to the Jews and even worshipped as Greek influence spread through the country—Zeus, the father of gods; Athene, goddess of wisdom; Aphrodite, of love; Apollo, sun-god of light and youth; Pan, of nature, goat-footed and playing his reed pipes; Ares, of war; Artemis, of hunting. The gods lived in power and majestic beauty on Mount Olympus. The Greeks had no room for ugliness; they worshipped beauty in all its forms—beauty of thought as well as of body. On the

through Tyre and Gaza, he marched to Egypt; then back he came, northwards into the Fertile Crescent, through Mesopotamia, conquering Babylon, Susa, Ecbatana (see map). Darius III, King of Persia, fled and was murdered, far away from his capital; Alexander's empire now reached from Greece to India.

He was a noble ruler, intent upon being "lawgiver to all and to reconcile humanity . . . in a single fatherland". Perhaps as one way of trying to do this, he took over the gods of the nations he defeated—Amen-Ra of Egypt, Melkart of Phoenicia, Merodach of Chaldea (Babylonia) and even Yahweh of the Jews. He founded many cities—Alexandria, Kandahar, Samarkand, all self-governing and settled by Greeks, Jews and Persians alike, but Greek in pattern and ideals.

This is a carving of Greek warriors going to war. They carry circular shields. Look closely at their helmets.

Three Greek gods, Poseidon, Apollo, Artemis. What did each represent to the Greeks?

gods depended their crops, their safety on long journeys by sea and on land, their victory in war; every house had its shrine and altar at which daily prayers and gifts were offered. Four times a year feasts and holidays were celebrated before the shrine of Zeus, and every fourth year the famous Olympic Games were held. The Greeks' intense love of games, athletics, drama and pageantry led to the building of huge theatres and arenas, circular and tiered so that everyone could see and hear; many of these were built in Palestine.

A Divided Empire

The story of Greek rule after the death of Alexander does not, however, make pleasant reading. When news of his death came, the two chief leaders of his armies split the empire between them. Ptolemy I took over Egypt, with his capital at Alexandria, and ruled the Ptolemaic Empire. Seleucus took Asia, with his capital at Antioch, a new city fast becoming important in Syria; he changed his name to Antiochus I and ruled the Seleucid Empire. Ptolemy and Seleucus soon quarrelled over Palestine. Once more the land lay between two great nations, like a lamb between two hungry lions. In 312 B.C. Ptolemy captured Jerusalem and his empire held Judah

for over a hundred years; then the Seleucid Empire completely defeated the Egyptians (see Dan. xi) in 198 B.C., and Judah came under the rule of yet another nation.

There were feuds, wars and murders until Rome overtook both empires. The Jews had stayed submissive under Greek rule; Jerusalem had become the cultural and religious centre for the Jews scattered throughout the land, and the scribes and writers had done much to continue the records of the country's history.

The Septuagint

Some of the Jews of the Dispersion, you will recall, were in Egypt, and had forgotten both their native Hebrew and colloquial Aramaic. They spoke Greek. (We remember here that the New Testament was written in Greek.) It soon became necessary for them to have their Law in Greek too. In Alexandria, Ptolemy II invited seventy scribes (or so the story goes) to come and translate the five books of the Law—the Pentateuch—into Greek. The High Priest sent six men from each of the twelve tribes. There are several accounts of the magical way in which each of the seventy-two scholars produced on the Island of Pharos identical translations, but the main thing for us to remember is that this work gave us the

Septuagint—often written LXX and meaning Seventy. This was done in 250 B.C. and as time went on other parts of what we now know as the Bible were added; this Greek Bible was read in all the synagogues outside Palestine, and in this way it is to Alexander the Great that the world owed the holy scriptures in a tongue that everybody could understand. It meant that people who were not Jews—i.e. Gentiles—could read and hear about God in the Greek tongue, and they could even become members of the synagogues if they believed in Yahweh. Paul found many of these Gentile believers in his missionary journeys when he visited synagogues in cities of Asia Minor and in Greece itself.

The Rosetta Stone

It is a later Pharaoh—Ptolemy V—to whom we owe further light on the history of this time. In about 196 B.C. he approved a decree proclaimed by the priests of Memphis. To make sure that everybody understood it he had it inscribed on a huge slab of black basalt in three languages

The disc-thrower, perhaps the most beautiful example of Greek art and athletic skill. Disc-throwing is still part of the Olympic Games.

—in Egyptian hieroglyphics or picture-writing, in the common written language of the people and in Greek. In A.D. 1799 it was discovered at Rosetta, to the west of the Nile delta, and from this famous Rosetta Stone scholars have been able to translate all the Egyptian hieroglyphics for the first time, because they could read the Greek and compare the two (see Book I, p. 40). It is a wonderful experience to stand quietly in front of this stone—not unlike a rather chipped black gravestone—and to think about the people who wrote it, read it and discussed it; and we are glad that Greek became the "official" language of the people in those days, for we realise that because of this we can also read unknown tongues which our scholars for so many years could not interpret.

Religious Differences

The Jews were not long left to their quiet existence. There had been some disagreement over taxes, and quarrels quickly broke out over these. But there were differences of opinion in their worship too, and a certain amount of bitterness resulted from religious arguments and beliefs. Surrounded by Greek colonies, some of the Jews began to accept Greek thought and religion. They began to believe in "another world" and life after death—what we sometimes call "immortality". In Book I there is a drawing of the Hebrew Universe showing Sheol, the abode of the dead. Most of the Jews believed that when people died their spirits went to this place and were forever lost (see Ps. vi, 5). Now the Greeks were making them think about a place where life went on; Greek legends of Spring have this thought behind them. Of course, these ideas were not as clear then as they were after the teachings of Jesus, but you can see how the people would certainly argue and even quarrel over the possibilities and beliefs about life-after-death, as they do today. Two sects of Jews were already showing differences in their religion—the Pharisees and Sadducees; the Pharisees held that the really important part of worship was the keeping of the Law; the Sadducees, although priests, refused to have anything to do with the idea of an after-life.

Desecration of the Temple

Then came a disastrous event. In 168 B.C.

In Athens stands a wonderful temple—the Parthenon, a glorious example of the kind of architecture brought to Palestine by the Greeks.

Antiochus Epiphanes, a hated ruler, found some of the Jews plotting against the High Priest whom he had chosen to be in charge of the Temple. Then and there he decided to stamp out altogether the worship of Yahweh and to hellenise (make Greek) the Jewish religion. He even called himself a god: "Epiphanes" meant "the god manifest" or revealed. He made up his mind to introduce Greek gods to replace Yahweh and that the Jews must accept *his* religion whether they liked it or not. He murdered the priests, entered the Temple, plundered its contents and burned the Law books; he even walked right through the Holy of Holies, desecrating it in the eyes of the Jews. He carried away the Temple vessels of gold and silver, the seven-branched candlestick, the golden altar and the rich draping curtains of scarlet, together with the priests' garments. 1 Macc. i, 20 ff. describes this, and in iv, 38 we read that the sanctuary was laid desolate, the gates were destroyed, the priests' apartments were razed until there were "shrubs growing in the courts as in a forest or as on one of the mountains".

Most dreadful deed of all, the king offered swine—an insult to the Jews themselves—to himself in the form of Zeus the Greek god, on Yahweh's altar. Orders went out to all cities and villages in Judaea (as it is now called) to do likewise, and the Jews in their desperation looked for someone to lead them. Antiochus was anxious about the nearness of Roman legions at this time and with his armies prevented Jewish people from free movement, trading and even worship; he did not realise that because of his tyranny he was not breaking Jewish opposition; that, in fact, he was strengthening it into a revolt for religious freedom.

Revolt!

The spark was kindled in a tiny village called Modin, lying in the hills between Jerusalem and Joppa. An old priest named Mattathias refused to obey the command to sacrifice to the Greek gods; he slew another priest who was willing to do so, as well as the watching Greek officer, then destroyed the defiled altar and fled with his five sons to the hills. There they began a guerrilla warfare. On a sabbath some of them were caught and according to their laws refused to fight; they were massacred (1 Macc. ii, 36). From this time the rebels fought for their religious faith even on

ΕξΗΛΘΕΝΔΕ ΒΑCΙΛΕΥCCΟΔΟΜωΝΕΙCΥΝΑΝ
ΤΗCΙΝ ΑΥΤωΜΕΤΑΤΟΫΠΟCΤΡΕψΑΙΑΥΤΟΝ
ΑΠΟΤΗCΚΟΠΗCΤΟΥΧΟΔΑΛΛΟΤΟΜΟΡΚΑΙ
ΤωΝΒΑCΙΛΕωΝΤωΝΜΕΤΑΥΤΟΥΕΙCΤΗΝ
ΚΟΙΛΑΔΑ ΤΗΝCΑΥΗ· ΤΟΥΤΟΗΝΤΟΠΕΔΙΟΝ
ΒΑCΙΛΕωΝ· ΚΑΙΜΕΛΧΙC ΕΔΕΚ ΒΑCΙΛΕΥC
ΣΑΛΗΜΕξΗΝΕΓΚΕΝΑΡΤΟΥCΚΑΙΟΙΝΟΝΗΝ
ΔΕΪΕΡΕΥCΤΟΥΘ̄ῩΤΟΥΥψΙCΤΟΥ· ΚΑΙΕΥΛΟΓΗ
CΕΝΤΟΝΑΒΡΑΜ ΚΑΙΕΙΠΕΝ· ΕΥΛΟΓΗΜΕΝΟC

This is a specimen of early Greek writing from the Septuagint (LXX). It is Gen. xiv, 17. The New Testament was written in Greek, the language common to eastern countries at this time.

the sabbath. Antiochus thought that this kind of rebellion would soon be put down, but he did not realise the kind of people he was attempting to destroy. The Jews now had a new leader, Judas Maccabaeus—the "Hammerer" (1 Macc. iii, 1–4); he believed that "with heaven it is all one, to save by many or by few, for victory in battle standeth not in the multitude of a host; but strength is from heaven".

He made his centre at Mizpah and prepared to stand against much larger and stronger forces of Syrian soldiers. With his four brothers he harried the enemy and gained considerable ground, even defeating an army supported by troops of elephants (1 Macc. ii, 4 ff.). By 164 B.C. he was in a strong position, and although he could not take the Acra, a fortress near the Temple, he entered Jerusalem, cleansed the Temple and restored it, then rededicated it to the worship of Yahweh. The Jews still celebrate this great event, calling it the Feast of Dedication or the Feast of Lights (John x, 22). Freedom for the Jewish religion was almost won. But Judas was not satisfied. He was very ambitious and he wanted to extend his conquests; but he was brutal and savage enough to embitter not only his enemies and those Jews who had accepted the Greek form of worship, but also some of his own people who were satisfied with what had so far been achieved; amongst these were the Pharisees, the Chasidim or "The Separated".

The Struggle Continues

The rulers of the Seleucid Empire also distrusted the success of Judas, although at first he was officially recognised as the governor of Judaea. Wars continued and four years later Judas was killed. His brothers went on with the struggle and somehow through all the strife managed to throw off taxes and get rid of military control in the Acra, which was razed to the ground (1 Macc. xiii, 41 ff.).

A new line of priest-kings had by now come into Jewish history; descended from Mattathias, these were called the Hasmoneans. But a new Seleucid king took a firm hand and besieged Jerusalem yet again; he destroyed its walls, demanded tribute and turned out the High Priest. The great hope of the Hasmoneans had been to extend Judaea to the sea-coast, but she was once more a vassal state and under the Seleucids for the next ten years. Then the High Priest seized a new chance and for sixty years gave religious and political freedom to the Jews. The dream of power was revived and the Hasmoneans extended their kingdom by forcing their neighbouring states one by one under the rule of Judaea. The Seleucids were anxious about Rome at this time, and were too much concerned with their northern lands to worry much about the Jews.

Pharisees and Sadducees

The High Priest, John Hyrcanus, nephew of Judas Maccabaeus, was now openly calling himself King; he even had a bodyguard as David had when he was king. There followed a bewildering series of squabbles and fightings amongst the king's family, and religious differences grew stronger than ever as the Pharisees and Sadducees argued about how the people should worship.

Greek artists took great delight in beautifying their vases with pictures of daily life, wars and games, or merely in fanciful designs.

The Pharisees kept strictly to the Law, especially its teachings interpreted by the scribes; they paid their Temple dues regularly and in the same formal way set up rules and regulations of their own making. In later years it was these petty laws that aroused the scorn of Jesus (Matt. xxiii). But they did try to serve Yahweh honestly and they also believed in the resurrection—or, at least, some kind of after-life. The Sadducees, on the other hand, held to the Law of Moses only and denied an after-life. They were inclined to accept Greek rites in their worship and this angered the Pharisees, who wanted to keep the worship of Yahweh traditionally Jewish and free from any kind of change.

Civil War!

There came a day when a new High Priest so angered the people by his slackness in carrying out his duties that they pelted him with the citrons and lemons they had brought with them as part of their offerings. He brought out his bodyguard and there was fighting and bloodshed. For six years civil war continued; then the Pharisees asked the Seleucid king to come and help them; but some of the army deserted and the Pharisees were defeated. The Sadducee High-Priest-King took control once more. Tradition says that he crucified Jewish captives—mostly Pharisees—and murdered their families whilst the Sadducees looked on. This was an almost unbelievable cruelty to be ordered by a High Priest of the Temple. The people were in utter dejection and weary of war. More than ever did they long for a divine leader, someone sent from God—a Messiah. We should remember that this Messiah did come; and many who watched Him on the cross must have recalled stories that their parents had told them—of those eight hundred crosses bearing Jewish captives; and there was a High Priest concerned in both events.

The Synagogue

Strange as it may seem, the Pharisees came into power a few years later, during the reign of a woman ruler (she could not be priest, of course). They set about educating the people in the Law by building synagogues and schools. Whereas the Temple had been the place for priests and sacrifice and ceremony, the synagogue could be used by everybody—including women, who sat behind a kind of lattice hidden from the men. There was no altar. A Rabbi—a teacher rather than a priest—led the service; he had to know a great deal about the Law and its teachings. The service consisted of a psalm (all joining in), prayers, two lessons—one from the Law and one from the Prophets—and a spoken explanation of some of the passages, a kind of sermon. The chief work of the scribes was to interpret the Law in such a way that it meant something to the people

This painting of a lady and her servant is to be found on a Greek vase.

Greeks trampling out grapes: compare this with the Jews' use of the winepress on p. 45.

in any country or province where there was a synagogue; we must not forget that originally the Law had been given to the Israelites when they were in the Wilderness, and now that the people were living in villages and cities some parts of the Law did not really apply to them. The Law itself is often called the *Torah*. Some of the scripture passages were translated from the Hebrew into the common Aramaic tongue so that the people could understand them better; these translations were called *Targums*.

The Synagogue Scriptures

We recall how the Priestly writers had guided the scribes in the weaving into history of the familiar stories of the patriarchs and judges and kings. Not caring to leave out any of the old stories, they took all the accounts written in the Northern Kingdom in about 750 B.C. (the time of Amos) and called E, because E stands for Elohim, a name for God, and joined them, story for story, to the similar accounts written in the Southern Kingdom in about 850 B.C. (the time of Elisha) and called J, because J stands for Jahveh, another way of spelling Yahweh (see p. 35).

These accounts had undergone all sorts of changes and alterations through the years, especially during the Exile, when the Priests revised them to fit their own ideas and way of thinking about God and His people; these were the P documents—P standing for Priests, or Priestly Code. The scriptures, as given by Ezra to the people, then consisted of the Law and the Prophets, plus stories of their leaders. The Writings, a third section of the Old Testament as we have it, came when the Psalms and similar collections of poetry were added. These were the scriptures of the Pharisees of the Dispersion in Palestine, Egypt and Asia Minor, and translated into the Greek Septuagint (LXX); they were written on papyrus rolls or prepared skins and kept in a special cupboard called an ark. (Do not confuse this with the Ark of the Covenant.)

Next to the synagogue was a school where boys were taught to read and learn by heart passages of the scriptures; this explains why Jesus had such a full knowledge of the "Law and the Prophets".

The power of the Pharisees came to an end when the Sadducees, who had been jealous of their rule, of course, supported a new High-Priest-King who tried to take control and to rule over not only Judaea but also Edom, Galilee and

Some coins of Alexander the Great, Seleucus I of Syria, and Ptolemy of Egypt. These were known and used by the Jews under these three rulers.

Samaria. Both sides now had armies and before long the country was again plunged into civil war.

A model in terra cotta of two Greek girls playing at knuckle bones, 300 B.C. No doubt Jewish girls played it too.

EXPRESSION WORK

1. Find out all you can about Aristotle. Why do we owe so much to this great Greek philosopher?
2. Find a Greek hero, philosopher, poet and orator, then prepare notes for a talk on each.
3. Write: "A Day in My Life", by a Greek lad.
4. What is the LXX? How was it made and why is it important?
5. Prepare a discussion between a Pharisee and a Sadducee on the possibility of an after-life.
6. Write a letter to a friend in Alexandria describing the desecration of the Temple by Antiochus Epiphanes.
   or
   The motto of Antiochus Epiphanes could have been "Might is Right". Why?
7. Act the refusal of Mattathias to offer sacrifice.
   or
   In a cave in the hills, let Mattathias and his five sons plan their future activities.
8. What is the Feast of Lights?
9. What was the belief of Judas about help from God?
10. Letter and learn a sentence you have noted in your reading.
11. Draw a map to show the Seleucid and Ptolemaic (Egyptian) Empires, at the time of Judas Maccabaeus.
12. The events of history in this chapter are found in 1 Macc. in the Apocrypha. What is the Apocrypha?

Studying the Roll of the Law in the synagogue exactly as boys did under the Pharisees in 200 B.C.

CHAPTER 12

THE ROMAN EMPIRE AND HEROD THE GREAT

(1 Macc. viii; selected Psalms; 1 Chron. xvi; Ecclus. 1, 5–21)

THE struggle between the Pharisees and the Sadducees continued. By now, Roman legions were marching into Syria as the kings of the Seleucid Empire had feared would happen; Pompey took over the empire. He set up his headquarters at Antioch and later went southwards to settle the quarrels between the two Jewish sects. Suspicious of the Sadducees, who supported their own Priest-King in any attempt at rebellion against the ruling power, Pompey, in 63 B.C., besieged Jerusalem. He attacked on a sabbath day and the defenceless priests went on with their normal duties, knowing full well that they would be murdered as they did so.

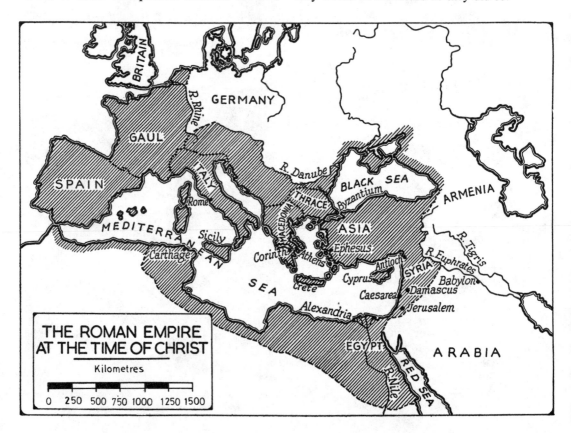

Notice how the new empire of Rome has moved towards the West, engulfing the traders of Phoenicia and Carthage; thus, the spread of the Gospel by Paul, to Europe, was made easy. Roman soldiers brought Christianity to England.

The Jews learned bitterly to recognise a Roman soldier; but read Eph. vi, 13-17.

that Rachel stole hers when she and Jacob left Laban. The gods that looked after the farm were called lares; those that preserved the home, penates. They could bring good or bad fortune and unless they were given the honour due to them the family fell on evil days. Therefore, in every house there was a shrine on which were offered fruit, flowers and wine; then prayers were said. There were special occasions, too, when the gods were taken round the fields and sacrifices were offered. Jupiter and Juno were the chief gods; Minerva, goddess of wisdom; Mars, god of war; Vesta, goddess of fire. Many of these were Greek gods with Roman names; thus, the Roman Jupiter and Zeno were the Greek Zeus and Hera. The Jews were tempted to worship these gods, as their forefathers had been when under the influence and power of Assyria and Babylonia; and since the Romans themselves had

Pompey did not defile the Temple, nor did he interfere with the religious freedom of the Jews. But he joined Judaea to Syria and demanded both tribute and loyalty from the people. Strife still continued between the High Priest's party and the Pharisees, however, and there were minor outbreaks against the Romans too. At last, in 54 B.C., the rebellions were crushed by Cassius (murderer of Julius Caesar) and many thousands of Jews were sold into slavery, some being taken to Rome: this indirectly extended the Dispersion to Europe.

Roman Worship

But Caesar allowed more freedom to the Jews than had Pompey; he reduced the taxes and agreed to the rebuilding of the walls of Jerusalem. There is no doubt that the soldiers and citizens of Rome who settled in the district brought with them their own gods and forms of worship. Like the Hebrews of old, they had their terra-cotta teraphim or household gods—you will remember

Jupiter (Jove), the chief Roman god—of thunder and storms and justice. This statue was found in the temple at Palmyra, a trading centre of Roman Syria. He is armed with thunderbolts and attended by eagles.

Mithras was a Persian god accepted in 68 B.C. as the god of light, strength and Roman soldier's honour. A temple to Mithras has been found in London. How do you account for this?

Roman Writing

We owe our letters to the Romans too; the print at which you are now looking is Roman lettering. The Bible references throughout this book are given in Roman numerals, most of which are easy to read with a little practice. The use of C, D and L often gives more difficulty. The Romans showed 1,000 by a circle O, 500 by half a circle Ɔ D, 100 by a half-circle without the diameter C, and 50 by the lower half of this, ∟, which soon became more like an L. The 1,000 later became shown as twice 500, i.e. by two semicircles—Ɔ and D; if you put these two close together they make ƆD or Φ, = M. Instead of writing four X, i.e. XXXX, for 40, they made it ten less than 50—XL; for 60, ten more than 50—LX. You will remember that the Septuagint, written by seventy scholars, was and still is shown as LXX.

a strong sense of loyalty to their gods, it is more than likely that these Jews accepted Roman gods alongside their own Yahweh. Mithras, god of light and strength, was worshipped even in England, and a temple to this god has been excavated in London. We shall hear more of both Greek and Roman gods and their influence upon the Jews of the Dispersion in Book IV.

Roman boys at school did their writing in a similar way to that done by the Greeks. A wooden tablet was covered with wax and with a pointed instrument—a sharpened reed, for instance—they wrote or scratched their work into the wax. Warming the wax would enable them to "rub out" and prepare the tablet for further work. If longer exercises or letters were to be written, these were done on parchment

An example of Roman work — an aqueduct. Note the Roman arches.

The Romans built a Forum in each large city where people could gather to hear and discuss and exchange ideas. This is part of the enormous circle at ancient Jerash, east of the Jordan, centre of caravan routes.

made from papyrus—of which we read in Book I. A reed pen was sharpened and dipped into ink made from soot-black and gum. The ink bottle was a small cylinder in shape with a conical top. The writing was done in columns and the papyrus was unrolled to the right and rolled from the left as it was read. Rolls to be kept—those of the great orators like Cicero—were put into a kind of drum-shaped box with a hinged lid.

The Calendar

An interesting story of Roman origin concerns the calendar, the first of which, made by Romulus, contained ten months relating to the periods of the moon. The names of the months were those of Roman gods and goddesses—perhaps you can guess some of these. Julius Caesar improved on this in 46 B.C., and July was named in his honour. We also have the month of August, after Augustus Caesar of whom we shall hear shortly. But the story of the calendar must be followed elsewhere.

Roman Rule

Caesar's freedom to the Jews probably arose from the fact that the Romans believed in allowing conquered nations to manage their own affairs so long as they remained loyal to Rome and did not join with other nations to rebel; they were to regard themselves as Romans and could earn the right to be Roman citizens, with all the advantages of such freedom. We know that Paul was proud of the fact that he was "free-born" (see Book IV).

In order to encourage in the conquered people the idea of their being Roman, all sorts of Roman ideas were introduced to them. We have already seen the influence of their god-worship and language—though we must admit the greater influence of the Greek tongue, which continued

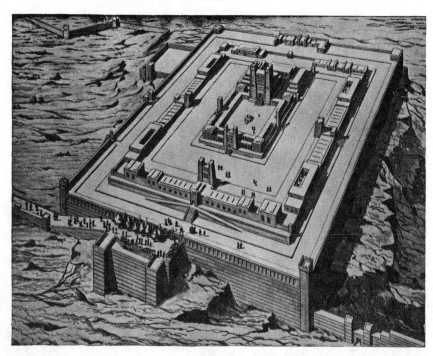

What Herod the Great's Temple in Jerusalem may have looked like. The centre court was for the priests only; the tallest tower marks the Holy of Holies.

to be used in trade and argument. Fine roads were made to take the place of the winding caravan routes, cities were walled, aqueducts for water transport were raised, heating and drainage were improved. Even more important, perhaps, was the setting-up of Roman customs of rule, by which the Jews had the right to consider, discuss and pass laws benefiting their own people. But the Romans had little time for beauty as loved by the Greeks. They were hard-headed, practical, disciplined and to some extent unimaginative. The art they did practise was for the most part copied from the Greeks.

Herod the Great

We now hear about Herod the Great. In 40 B.C. Rome found that Syria was being invaded by the Parthians, who had promised to help the Jews too, if they wished to rebel against Caesar. Herod had been in power for some time, even then, but now fled to Rome. He returned three years later, in 37 B.C., with an army, captured Jerusalem and became the first King of the Jews. His rule was difficult, for the Jews hated him, as they did all foreigners. He was an Edomite, whose father Antipater had left his country to the south of the

Dead Sea (once the home of Esau) to lead the Jews through an anxious period of their history; but the Jews had shown no gratitude, and as far as they were concerned Antipater could have gone back to Edom, and Herod with him. Herod did not receive much help from Rome either. Antony, the new Caesar, was under the spell of Cleopatra, the last ruler of the Ptolemy dynasty of Egypt, and had little interest in the rule of Herod. But Herod made no secret of his plans to be absolute king; he was determined to be without a rival, to the extent of murdering all his enemies, including the High Priest, and took sides with the Pharisees, as most of the successful rulers before him had done.

On the defeat and death of Antony and Cleopatra in a Roman civil war, Octavian became the new ruler of the Roman Empire and, under the name of Augustus, the first Emperor of Rome. Peace seemed likely to last for many years and during this period—known as the Pax Romana (Roman peace)—Herod went over to Augustus to make sure of Roman protection and help should he need it. The emperor accepted Herod, seeing in him a man on whom he could rely for firm control of Judaea. Herod was thus certain

The High Priest wearing his breastplate and carrying a censer. By the time of Jesus he was absolute ruler of the religious lives of the people, and his friendship with Rome made him powerful even in their civil lives.

even love. It is not surprising that the Jews scattered throughout the then known world returned to Jerusalem whenever they could to see their Temple and to worship there the God of all Israel. The drawing of this Temple should be closely compared with that of the magnificent Temple of Solomon shown in Book I; it will then be seen how different the buildings were in size and style but how much alike in actual shape and plan.

Its Extent

In order to make sure that the Temple had a sound foundation, the top of Mt. Moriah was built up, so that underneath the Temple were large crypts and rooms for storage; even horses were stabled there.

The whole site measured about 400 metres by 300 metres. The main entry was through the Golden Gate; the doors were massive and covered with brass, twenty men being needed to open and shut them. This gate led to the Court of the Gentiles, beyond which any who were not Jews

of Roman support and continued to strengthen his own position in the country.

Herod's Troubles

It is not surprising to learn that he had a good deal of trouble in his home and palace, for he had ten wives! They seem to have spent a great deal of their time in fighting, quarrelling and plotting. Herod met these troubles with murder and execution—even of members of his own family. He was determined to let no one, not even his wives, interfere with his rule over the Jews.

Yet Palestine began to grow powerful once more. Herod built good roads and stamped out robber bands. New cities, like Caesarea and Samaria—which had been razed to the ground years before—were built; others were fortified. He made Samaria his northern capital and built there a Roman amphitheatre like the one shown in Book III. More important to our story than all, however, was the rebuilding of the Temple.

The Temple

Begun in 20 B.C., it was not finished even in Christ's time (John ii, 16–20 and Mk. xiii, 1). The architecture was Grecian, in white marble, "like a mountain covered with snow". Gates and pillars were overlaid with gold, and as it glittered in the bright sunshine it must have given every Jew a great sense of pride and happiness and

A Jewish lamp, showing the Menorah (seven-branched lampholder)—see Ex. xvii, 12; xxv, 31, 32. There is a shofar and a shovel used in Temple sacrifices.

The Wailing Wall of Jerusalem. It is now a shrine and place of prayer for Jews and is the only remaining portion of the original walls of Herod's Temple.

could not go; across it was a wall of marble, 1·4 m high, on which in Greek and Latin were the words: "No foreigner may enter within the screen and enclosure round the Holy Place. Whosoever is caught so trespassing will himself be the cause of death overtaking him." A polite way of saying: "Trespassers will be executed!"

Through the Beautiful Gate was the Court of the Women, where was also the Treasury, containing thirteen trumpet-mouthed chests for offerings; each chest was for some special purpose and the giver could chose any one for his gifts. This Court was as far as women were allowed to go. Beyond this was the Gate of Nicanor, leading into the Court of the Men; thence to the Court of the Priests, where the service and sacrifices of the priests at the four-horned Altar of Burnt Offering could be seen, and where the Temple choir and musicians led the psalms and singing.

The Temple itself was small, beautiful and sacred. No actual service took place within it. Before it reared a huge porch 52·5 m high and broad; the Holy Place was 36·5 m wide, its

double doors being covered with a veil of rich Babylonian material in purple and blue. The priest entered only during the hours of duty; here were the Table of Shewbread, the Menorah—a golden candlestick with seven branches—and the Altar of Incense. Beyond was the Holy of Holies, empty except for a stone representing the lost Ark of the Covenant (see Book I). The Holy of Holies, separated from the Holy Place by only a veil of beautiful material, was entered but once a year, and then only by the High Priest on the Day of Atonement; on this occasion he spoke aloud the Sacred Name of Yahweh.

Its Music—the Psalms

During the period of the Maccabees, the hymn-book of the Temple was being put together—compiled, as we say. Psalms had been written for many years before this time, some of them by David himself; these were in Book 1 and consisted of Psalms i–xli. Then, about 300 B.C., Books 2 and 3 were collected, containing Psalms

A selection of Roman coins. These had to be exchanged for Temple shekels when the Jews paid their religious dues.

A silver shekel dating from 138 B.C. It bears the facade of the Temple and the word "Simon". On the reverse is a lulav—a bundle of palm branches, and an ethrog —a citrus fruit; these were symbols of the Feast of Tabernacles. The words are "For the Freedom of Jerusalem".

xlii–lxxxix. During the last two hundred years B.C., and including the time the Temple was begun, other psalms were written, and put into Books 4 and 5. The collected psalms are called the *Psalter*.

They tell in beautiful language the story of the Jews—their fears and hopes, sadness and joy. There are psalms of thanksgiving, praise and worship in honour of God the Creator Who is righteous and just and holy. These psalms were sung in Temple worship and varied according to the day of the week. In the intervals between the groups of verses, the priests blew their trumpets and the people fell prostrate before the altar (Ps. cl). The Temple orchestra played on wind instruments like rams' horns and pipes, stringed instruments like psalteries and harps, percussion, such as cymbals, timbrels and tambourines. In Herod's Temple there was an organ with thirteen pipes and two bellows. Both men and boys sang in the choir and there was also dancing (Ps. cxlix). Some of the psalms contained responses sung by the choir and people in reply to the leader or priest, e.g. Ps. cxlv and cl. These are called antiphonal psalms.

Special psalms were sung on special occasions, e.g. Ps. cxxxv at the Feast of Dedication. The "Songs of Degrees", Ps. cxx–cxxxiv, were probably sung by pilgrims on their way to Jerusalem for the feasts.

When reading some of the psalms you will come across the word "selah". It marks the end of a group of verses and is believed to indicate in the singing of the psalms some change in musical accent, rhythm or tempo. It certainly should not be read aloud when you are reading the psalms in school or church, any more than you would say "full-stop" at the end of this sentence.

In Psalm cl is a list of musical instruments used in the Temple. The psaltery was a harp, and the harp then used was more like the lyre.

Haggai ii, 9 summed up the feelings of the Jews about their Temple of 516 B.C. Herod's Temple was even more glorious, especially when we realise that it was the Temple into which Jesus went for worship during His life and ministry.

Nearby was the Castle of Antonia, a stronghold for the Roman soldiers whose duty it was to keep guard over the city and to deal with possible riots and signs of rebellion. They had also to enforce law and order in the collecting of the hated taxes and levies demanded by Caesar.

"In the Days of Herod the King"

Despite the great care Herod took over the building of the Temple, he was not popular with either the Jews or the Romans. He had hoped to reconcile the Pharisees and the Sadducees, but angered them all when he reared over the Temple the Roman eagle itself. The deeply religious Jews openly sneered at him—"this foreigner"—and the Romans thought of him as an upstart. He loved pomp and ceremony and probably saw himself as another Solomon. He imitated the Greeks by introducing their athletics and pageantry; this further upset the religious sects, who said that such things were wicked and against the laws of Yahweh. Some of the older members, too, must have been horrified at seeing the younger priests hurry over their duties at the Temple in order to rush to the arena and gymnasium to join in the excitement provided there. Herod also built fortresses to strengthen his position, but this made the Romans suspicious that he was plotting against them. He then tried to win favour by calling one city after the emperor himself—Caesarea. His reign was full of murders and cruelty of all kinds, for he was constantly afraid of his enemies. A dread disease (we do not know what it really was) took hold of him and this made his fear even more frightening to him; he became so brutal and savage that he could order the deaths of tiny babies.

He died in 4 B.C., a frightened, miserable man. But into the world, "in Bethlehem of Judaea in the days of Herod the King", had come the Child he could not kill, the Child sent by God Himself to become the King of all mankind—Jesus Christ, our Lord.

EXPRESSION WORK

1. What benefits did Rome bring to Judaea, and which of these eventually reached England?
2. Find out all you can about Herod the Great.
3. Pretend you are a Jewish lad attending the new Temple for the first time. Describe all you see and hear. Ecclesiasticus l, 5–21 (in the Apocrypha) will help you.
4. Write Haggai ii, 9 in your own words.
   or
   Ps. cxix is an acrostic psalm. What does this mean?
5. Make a model of the Temple, from any suitable material.
6. What are lares and penates? How do they compare with the teraphim of the Israelites?
7. A Jew from Jerusalem meets a friend in Caesarea. Write or act their conversation about the new Temple.
8. Draw a Roman soldier on guard.
9. To what extent were the Jews ready for a Messiah? What kind of a Person did they hope would appear?
10. (a) The word "Chasidim" is often used in connection with the Pharisees. Find out what it means and how it arose.
    (b) Find the origin of the word "Sadducees". Give talks to the class on the information you have found.
11. On Herod's death the land was divided among his three sons. Archelaus became ethnarch of Judaea, Samaria and Idumaea; Antipas tetrarch of Galilee, Peraea and land east of the Jordan; Philip tetrarch of the land east and north of the Sea of Galilee. Draw a map to show these kingdoms. What was an ethnarch and a tetrarch?
12. Letter and learn Isa. ix, 6 (omit the comma in Wonderful, Counsellor). Learn Isa. lv.
    or
    Prepare for antiphonal reading in Morning Assembly, Psalm cxxxvi. What hymn would be suitable on this occasion?

THE WALLS OF JERUSALEM

The many walls of Jerusalem are not easy to trace and it is difficult to show them with real exactness. Note how the three valleys cut into the hills of the city.

CHAPTER 13

STORIES OF BABYLON AND PERSIA: DANIEL AND ESTHER

Daniel i, 8–21; ii, 1–19, 25–49; iii; v; vi. Esther iii–x)

DANIEL

THE Book of Daniel was written about 165 B.C., when Antiochus Epiphanes was carrying out his cruel persecutions of the Jews. It was written to encourage them to stand strong in their faith and belief that Yahweh was still with them and would see them through all their dangers and difficulties and distress under the rule of the Seleucid Empire; if the Jews withstood Antiochus he would never succeed in hellenising their religion as he had determined.

The Four Friends

To most of us these are familiar stories—about Daniel, Shadrach, Meshach and Abednego—and we should remember that they *are* stories. The original names of the friends were Daniel, Ananias, Misael and Azarias, but their Babylonian or Chaldean names are the more familiar

to us, although we do not use Daniel's new name, Belteshazzar, very frequently. If you look at the names closely you can see their connections with Babylonian gods—Bel, Aku and Nebo.

After the first siege of Jerusalem in 597 B.C., Nebuchadrezzar took captive all the courtiers, leaders and craftsmen of the city. Amongst these first captives were the four boys chosen by the king for special training and education in the Babylonian arts of war, hunting and leisure. They learned the Chaldean tongue and how to read and write the wedge-shaped cuneiform script. They learned how to count. The Babylonians counted in 60's rather than in 100's, and from them we have today our 60 seconds = 1 minute and 60 minutes = 1 hour.

The friends learned, too, how to behave in the king's court. Whatever they learned of Babylonian idol-worship, however, they held to their

Nebuchadrezzar was a great builder but these ruins are all that is left of his wonderful palace.

The Lion of Babylon, sculptured from the rock and found in the ruins of the city. It is supposed to mark the site of the Lion's Den in the stories of Daniel.

own Jewish faith in Yahweh and in the promise of Jeremiah that one day the people of Judah would return. It was because they wanted to keep their own laws that Daniel persuaded the king's steward to let them have water and vegetable foods rather than strong wine and meat that had been offered to idols or not killed in accordance with their laws (see, too, 1 Macc. i, 41–53).

Knowledge of the Stars

In chapter ii we learn that Daniel had a special interest in astrology and magic, as had Moses and Joseph years before. It was quite a common training for those who showed interest in the stars. In Babylonia the clear night skies were filled with brilliant stars that attracted the curiosity of scholars and lesser men like sorcerers and magicians, who, as members of the king's court, were expected to interpret movements of the stars as well as strange dreams.

Apart from the belief that fortunes could be "told from the stars"—astrology—there was in Babylonia a considerable knowledge of the stars and planets as a science—astronomy. Of course, the stars were linked with many legends of the Babylonian gods. The Moon was the father of the Sun and stars which shone and gleamed in the dry atmosphere of the country. The Sun's path was divided into twelve and stars were grouped into each division. Each month was controlled by a group of these stars, e.g. October by Scorpio (scorpion), April by Taurus (bull). Merodach was believed to have put the gods in their stations

"as the stars of the Zodiac" (Zodiac probably means "animals"). The Signs of the Zodiac have come down to us through the Phoenicians and the Greeks; they were certainly known by the Babylonians and by Daniel in his studies. You can find more about the Zodiac in reference books and encyclopaedias.

The King's Dream

When Nebuchadrezzar had his strange dream it was natural for him to send for his astrologers and soothsayers for an explanation of it; he made their task more difficult by forgetting what it was about. Daniel eventually interpreted it for him; he said that it was about an image and that a stone crashed on the feet of the image and broke it. The stone became a great mountain which filled the whole earth. This, said Daniel, meant that the dream foretold the rise and fall of many kingdoms but that in the end the kingdom of God would be supreme.

The king rewarded Daniel and his three friends, giving them high positions; Daniel was made a judge "at the gate"; he told the king that it was Yahweh Who had helped him to tell the king his dream and Nebuchadrezzar was tremendously impressed, so much so that he said, "Your God is the God of gods."

The Burning Fiery Furnace

You will recall how the Jews refused to worship

The Babylonians were much interested in astronomy and astrology and knew about the Signs of the Zodiac. Try to find out what each of these represents.

Dan. iii, 4, 5, lists some of the musical instruments played in Babylon. The harp or sackbut was possibly like this.

the figure of Zeus that Antiochus Epiphanes had raised on the altar of Yahweh. Chapter iii refers to the persecution of those who suffered for their faith and encourages them to resist a heathen religion. Nebuchadrezzar set up a golden image —probably of wood and covered with gold, standing sixty cubits high (a cubit was 46 to 51 centimetres). It was most likely erected to the glory of Merodach (Marduk), god of the wind, sun, thunder and life, his own god and "great lord". Daniel was away from the court on this occasion, perhaps on some ambassador's business for the king, but his three friends heard the herald's announcement and the king's decree that at the sound of music everybody had to worship the image; the three refused. (Amongst the listed instruments are the sackbut and psaltery, both triangular; the dulcimer was a stringed instrument; see drawing)

Nebuchadrezzar did not like to be disobeyed, but gave them another chance; they again refused. Then he threw them into the "burning fiery furnace". We know what happened and how even the king cried, "Blessed be the God of Shadrach, Meshach and Abednego!" when he learned of their safety. In the Apocrypha is the Song of the Three Holy Children which the three friends sang whilst in the fiery furnace. Its right-

ful place in the narrative appears to be between verses 23 and 24 of Dan. iii. You will also find this song as the Benedicite, in the Prayer Book.

The Writing on the Wall

The desecration of the Temple by Antiochus Epiphanes was still very much in the thoughts of the writer and in chapter v we find him foretelling disaster on those who defile the Holy Place. He tells of the King of Babylon drinking and feasting from the vessels stolen from the Temple; and he says that the nation will certainly meet destruction. The message to the Jews is clearly this—if such a king and his people are to be punished for stealing and defiling the vessels of the Temple, how much more certain will be the punishment of Antiochus Epiphanes who had committed sacrilege and even offered swine on Yahweh's altar.

The chapter as we have it is not strictly true history. Cyrus, not Darius, captured Babylon, and Belshazzar was son of the king then reigning and therefore a prince: but some scholars say that the prince may have been acting as regent at this time.

In the story the prince is horrified at the fingers of a hand that appear so strangely and write on the wall MENE, MENE, TEKEL, UPHARSIN. It is not certain what the words really meant; some say "counted, counted, weighed, divided"; others, "a mina, a mina, a shekel and half a mina", these being three weights representing the values of different kings of Babylon. Whatever they meant they carried with them the threat of doom. Babylon would fall, as Isaiah had foretold in xxxiv, 11–14.

Once again the message to the persecuted Jews is clear: they were to keep their faith and wait

The dulcimer is known to be an Eastern instrument like this. But some scholars think that the word in Dan. iii, 5 is a mistranslation of the Babylonian word for "bagpipe".

This lady is strumming the psaltery.

patiently for the fall of their enemies and the returning power of Yahweh.

Daniel in the Lions' Den

This is yet another story familiar to most of us (vi). Again there is a special message behind it, for the Jews. Following his desecration of the Temple, Antiochus tried to stamp out entirely the worship of Yahweh. He was determined to make all Jews worship Greek gods, and murdered the priests and ordered all Jews everywhere to do as he commanded. But this story tells the Jews quite clearly that whatever happened they must worship Yahweh faithfully, for He is the One True God.

The king's courtiers, jealous of Daniel, pre-pared a cunning plot into which the king fell. Having given an order, he could not change it; the "law of the Medes and Persians" was a decision that could not be altered. He therefore had to do as he had decreed, even though it meant the death of Daniel, who had been caught worshipping Yahweh at dawn, at 3 p.m. and at sunset, the Jews' hours of worship.

The lions' den was not far from the palace. Lions were kept in captivity ready to be released whenever the king wanted to go hunting, probably to make sure that he did not waste weary hours searching for them. When his seal—imprinted on wax or soft clay and sun-baked—had been fixed to the entrance, it was not possible for even the king himself to break it and release Daniel. But when he found that Daniel was still alive, he lost no time in flinging open the door to do so. As rulers of nations often did, he there-upon accepted Yahweh as a great God, and ordered his peoples to worship Him. Daniel was promoted to a high position.

ESTHER

The Book of Esther is a very fine story of plots and counter-plots in the Persian court. It should not be taken as true history and must be seen rather as a story that reveals bitter hatred against the heathen. There is nothing religious about it; it does not even mention God; and the Feast of Lots (Purim) it tells about is not written about anywhere else in the Bible.

A frieze found in Susa showing the bodyguard of Darius, some of the "Ten Thousand Immortals". They carried a bow, quiver and a spear with a silver pomegranate at one end. Their uniform was a wide-sleeved purple or yellow shirt, embroidered coat, turban of plaited reeds, laced shoes; they wore gold earrings and bracelets.

In Persepolis is a king's tomb carved on the cliff-face. Mazda flies overhead; the king and the altar of fire are borne on a platform on the shoulders of his subjects.

It is not easy to say why the book ever found its way into the Old Testament. Perhaps because it helps to explain the belief of the writer and the people that Israel could never be entirely destroyed whilst every Jew did his duty in standing up for his country—even if it meant risking his own life to do so.

Background and Plot

The story is set in Persia during the reign of Ahasuerus (Xerxes) about 485–465 B.C. The Feast of Lots (2 Macc. xv) became a yearly feast to keep in memory the deliverance from the Persians of the Jews then living in Persia; it may once have been a heathen feast adopted and altered by the Jews to fit their own celebrations. The author of the story lived about 130 B.C., when the successes of the Maccabaeans were filling the Jews with pride in their country. Judas Maccabaeus, you remember, had led the revolt against Antiochus, and for the next thirty years or so the Jews, despite feuds and quarrels between themselves, had thrown off much of the power of their rulers; the borders of Judaea had even been extended through conquest and force. But there was always the fear of being conquered again, and Roman power was stretching out its eagle's wings. It was necessary for every Jew to fight and risk death for his country.

The plot of the book tells how Queen Esther prevented the success of a cruel scheme planned by a courtier named Haman. He had made up his mind to destroy the Jews living in Persia. Haman, "a strutting little peacock", was furiously angry when the Queen's Jewish cousin Mordecai refused to bow to him or to pay him special respect. So Haman went to the king and, promising to pay 10,000 talents of silver, obtained the king's permission to slaughter the whole Jewish race on a day that he, Haman, would himself decide. The actual day was, in fact, postponed so that it fell on the 13th of the Jewish month Adar; this was the very day on which the Maccabees had defeated the Syrians in 135 B.C.

It is obvious that at the time Ahasuerus did not realise that his queen was a Jewess, or he might have thought twice about Haman's strange request. Haman erected an especially high gallows, hoping to see Mordecai swing for his "insults" to him. Esther knew it was a daring and dangerous thing to go to the king and ask him to change his decision. Once the king had made a decree it could not be altered. But she risked her life and pleaded for her people.

Ahasuerus decided to look into the court records, and found that he already owed his life to Mordecai, who had never been rewarded for saving it. Next morning, not knowing what was in store for him, Haman, secretly hopeful of power and reward, but seething with anger, led Mordecai clad in royal garments and on horseback through the city streets; for Haman had heard that "thus shall it be done unto the man whom the king shall delight to honour"—and whom should the king honour but Haman?

Then Esther begged for her people's safety and denounced Haman. Whereupon the king ordered that Haman be strung on the gallows he had raised for Mordecai, and Mordecai was given the high honours he had deserved (Ezra ii, 2; Neh. vii, 7).

Feast of Purim

But the king's decree was a "law of the Medes and Persians" and could not be changed. So he issued another decree in which the Jews were given permission for two days to defend themselves against the Persians who had been commanded to slay them. In so doing, they slew 75,800 Persians! The Feast of Purim was held to commemorate this deliverance. The word *purim* means "lots", because Haman had cast lots to decide upon the fatal day of the slaughter. From this time, all Jews were required to attend their synagogue and join in the reading of the Book of Esther from a roll—"The Roll"—containing just this one book; the feast following was one of rejoicing, mirth and revelry, to celebrate the joy of their ancestors' fortunate escape from cruelty and death.

EXPRESSION WORK

1. Why were these stories told?
2. Write and act a scene in which the four Jewish friends discuss their lives in Babylon.
    or
    What are the Twelve Signs of the Zodiac? What is their Babylonian origin?

3. Produce Dan. iii as a Dramatic Reading— you will need a Narrator, Herald, Chaldeans, Fearless Three, King and Counsellors.
4. Sketch some of the musical instruments mentioned in this chapter.
5. Write out and learn the verse you like best in the Benedicite.
6. Draw the scene of the "Writing on the Wall".
7. What is the "law of the Medes and Persians"? Illustrate it from the stories given you.
8. As jealous nobles of the court, plot against Daniel and draw up your request to put before the king.
9. What phrases tell us that the king was unhappy at having to carry out his decree?
    or
    What message about Yahweh did Darius send throughout his kingdom?
10. Why should Haman feel so bitter against the Jews as to want to slay them all?
11. Let Mordecai and Esther discuss their willingness to sacrifice their lives for Judaea and their countrymen.
12. "If I perish, I perish." What is the meaning of this cry?
    or
    Discuss whether or not you think the Book of Esther should be in the Old Testament part of our Bible.

The "Roll of Esther"— a beautiful illuminated copy of this separate scroll, read on the Feast of Purim a month before Passover.

CHAPTER 14

JOB AND JONAH

Job: R.V. advised—selected passages: i, 1–3, 6–22; ii, 1–7, 11, 13; iii, 1–19; iv, 7, 8, 17;
v, 17, 18; viii, 3, 5, 6, 20; xi, 6–9; xiii; xxii, 5–7, 9, 10; xxxi, 7–40; xxxviii, 1–12, 36; xxxix;
xl; xli; xlii, 1–12. Jonah i; ii, 1–10; iii; iv. Cf. Jer. xvi, 19; xviii, 3–12; Lk. xi, 29, 30. Isa. xlii,
6, 7; xlv, 14, 15; 2 Kings xiv, 26)

JOB

THE Book of Job was written about 500 B.C. We do not know the name of the author, but he was certainly a very fine poet. Like our own Shakespeare, he took as a framework an old story and turned it into a drama; like some of Shakespeare's plays, it has a prologue, a main plot and an epilogue. Its language is often beautiful.

The background of the story is the time of such patriarchs as Abraham and its theme or subject is the age-old problem: Why do good people suffer? Or as we sometime say: Why do cheats seem to prosper? or, Why do the wicked get on better than the good?

In the old story, Job was so good that one of God's "ministers", a kind of prosecutor called Satan (not the Tempter or the Devil, as he is sometimes called), asked God if he could test Job. He said Job was righteous merely because God was good to him and that if he were tried with many sorrows and losses he would turn against God. But Job bore his sufferings patiently and the Satan had to admit defeat; Job became even richer and worthier.

The Drama

Let us see what the poet makes of this old story. Job is "perfect and upright and one that feared God and shrank back from evil". ("Feared" does not mean that Job was afraid of God: he regarded God as great and wonderful and longed to worship and serve and work for Him.) Job is a wealthy sheikh or farmer in the Land of Uz—possibly on the borders of Syria, or even Edom down in the south; wherever it is, the hero does not appear to be an Israelite, which makes the story even more powerful, for Job is not one of the "chosen people". Every-

thing has so far gone well for him, and he is prosperous and happy. Then comes the Satan to God and says that Job is only good because he has all he needs. . . . "But touch all he hath and he will renounce Thee to Thy face," says the Satan. That is your task—to prove it, says God. So the Satan sets to work.

Everything now goes wrong for Job—there is murder, fire, storm, destruction of his servants, camels and home. He is ruined. Yet he does not blame God—that is the remarkable thing about Job. The Satan comes again to God, Who now gives him permission to make Job suffer physically, so long as he does not actually kill him. It is then that Job suffers dreadful boils—

An Arab sheikh of today. Job probably looked very much like him.

97

In the valley near Job's home women sifted the corn as they do today; a quiet, restful scene.

Job's sheep and goats grazed, too, as these do today; this is a modern picture of an ancient occupation.

a form of leprosy; his wife turns against him and against God; his friends come one by one and try to prove to him that he must have done some wicked thing in his past or secret life for God to punish him in this manner—in other words, that Job is getting what he deserves. This is almost a modern argument, that we get "what we deserve", but the kind of thing said usually by rather thoughtless and self-satisfied people. Job knows this is not true; he has no secret sin of which to be ashamed and he is patient in his miseries. But the doubt is put into his mind that God is not being very fair to him; at least He might have told him *why* he has had to suffer all these things, then they would have been easier to bear; perhaps his faith hasn't much foundation after all. He reaches the depth of disappointment and pessimism (ix, 23 and xiv, 1, 2).

"Job's Comforters"

His friends are "miserable comforters"; which is why today we speak of "Job's comforters". They are the kind of people who seem to enjoy the sorrows and sufferings of other people and feel how very good they themselves are; they are not very pleasant people. Job longs for someone to plead with God on his behalf, if only so that he can find out what is wrong and then he can put it right. This someone he calls a redeemer or vindicator—someone who will speak up for him. "I know that my redeemer liveth," he says. We are familiar with this cry because we have heard it sung in Handel's *Messiah*. This has perhaps altered its meaning for us, or at least the original meaning. Christ redeemed or saved us from *sin*, from wrong-doing, but Job had no sense of sin whatsoever, so he could not have been thinking of the resurrection as we think of it. In any case, he still believed in the old idea of the Hebrew heaven and Sheol, and had no thoughts of an after-life such as we learn from the life, death and rising again of Jesus. That idea had come very slowly to the Jews; the Pharisees, you will remember, began to believe in it, although the Sadducees refused to do so, and Jesus finally made it clear with His resurrection, for all to believe.

What is Man?

Job then demands: Has God really been fair to me? And God answers him, not in so many words, but by asking Job questions. One after another they come, all leading to the main demand: What can man do? Read xl, 6–14 and see that the only answer Job can give to all these questions is to admit that man is not really important, that he is very small and that God is very great. All creation is witness and proof of the wisdom of God, and man ought to trust Him at all times.

The Test of Faith

The drama ends almost too happily, for Job becomes even more prosperous than he was before his trials and temptations. Such an ending may mislead us in our final thoughts, if we are not careful. The poet is anxious to reward Job and to prove that by standing up to his test he received even greater riches. But real-life stories do not always end "happily ever after", as we well know. The real point of this story is Job's own faith and belief—that he has learned to trust God when everything goes wrong. It is easy enough to trust Him when "God's in His heaven; all's right with the world"; it is a much harder lesson to learn that He is just as near and ready to help when the "world is upside down". We may never have to suffer as Job did, but we all have to learn that sorrows and bitterness come to the best of people, and that the best of people stand strong in their faith in God and overcome them all.

Jonah tried to flee from Yahweh by boarding a ship from Joppa to Tarshish across the Mediterranean Sea. The cargo ship was Phoenician, like this. Read Ezek. xxvii.

The prophet went to Nineveh to preach to the Assyrians. He saw these palaces of the king.

JONAH

Here is yet another very fine old story of the Old Testament; this time it is a missionary story. There are people, of course, who believe that as it stands it is a true story, and there have been many arguments as to whether or not Jonah really was swallowed by a large fish, which these people insist upon calling a whale, although the word "whale" is not mentioned at all. It is a great pity that the point of the story is lost in these arguments, for there is a very fine underlying meaning to it that ought not be missed.

The author knew that one of the tasks given to Judah was to make Yahweh known to all the world, that is, to the heathen peoples, or as they were often called, the Gentiles. He also knew that the Exile had been in some part the punishment for not doing this task. He probably lived about 300 B.C., placing his story before the fall of both Assyria and Babylon. The story, as a kind of parable, seems to show that Jonah is the Jewish

Inside the palace is this hall with amazing sculptures and a golden ceiling. The king is entering, attended by a slave and his grand vizier; his musicians are playing hand harps. Note the Assyrian bull-gods.

nation, Nineveh the tyrant city representing the whole world, and the "great fish" the Exile or Captivity, from which Israel is "disgorged" in the Return.

Jonah Tries to Escape

Jonah is told that he has to go to Nineveh, the capital of the dreaded Assyrian Empire, to tell them about Yahweh. He refuses to go and, terrified, tries to get as far away from God as he can; this he does by boarding a cargo ship at Joppa, hoping to make for Tarshish (Tartessus), right across the Mediterranean in Spain, the furthest point of the then known world. Yahweh could not possibly reach him there. In the storm he learns that even the heathen are his brothers, despite their beliefs in gods other than his own; he is thrown overboard by the kindly yet fearful sailors, and then taken by the great fish "prepared to swallow up Jonah". There is nothing unusual in the Bible idea of being swallowed by a great fish; it is mentioned in Jer. li, 34, 44, Isa. xxvii, 1, and Ps. lxxiv, 13, where "dragon" = sea-monster. Here, it is the swallowing up of the Jewish nation by Babylonia. The author uses the phrase "three days and three nights", which is a Hebrew expression meaning "for a short time", after which Jonah is disgorged or thrown out; this is the release of Israel from exile.

Jonah Obeys

Ordered a second time, Jonah now obeys Yahweh and goes to preach in Nineveh. He is extraordinarily successful; even the king turns to Yahweh, Who tells Jonah that He forgives these people their wickednesses. But Jonah is angry at this; these people are not Yahweh's "chosen people", they cannot be spared from punishment. He has not yet learned that God loves all His people, however wicked they are and wherever they happen to live.

Jonah then builds a shelter or booth of branches as a protection against the hot sun. A gourd (possibly a wild vine) grows over it and serves for shade. It shrivels and dies, and Jonah is sorry to see that happen. God then says: "Thou hast pity for the gourd for which thou hast not laboured neither madest it grow; which came up in a night and perished in a night; should I not have pity on Nineveh, that great city?" That is, you are sorry for a plant that without any help from you grew and then died; don't you think I should be sorry for my people of Nineveh whom I brought into the world and whom I love? We are not told what Jonah said in reply, if he did reply; it is more than likely that when he saw what Yahweh meant he hung his head in silent shame. Perhaps, like the elder brother in Christ's story of the Prodigal Son, he had begun to learn

Part of the bronze band decorating the gates of the palace of Shalmaneser III, 860–825 B.C. **War chariots are advancing from the Assyrian camp. Jonah saw scenes like this.**

that God came not to seek the righteous but the lost. The real question is: will Israel carry out her task of bringing the heathen into God's Kingdom?

A Lesson to be Learned

But even by the time of Paul, the Jews had not learned this lesson; they still refused to listen to his plan to preach to the Gentiles (Acts xxii, 21 ff.). Isaiah had told the Jews that through them the Gentiles would be brought to Yahweh. But they remained jealous of their belief that having survived the Exile they were God's elect—his chosen people—and that no other nation could be as important as they. When would they learn that He was not merely the God of the Jews, but that He was God of the whole world?

EXPRESSION WORK

1. List ten of the questions Yahweh asks Job. What was the only answer Job could give? Why?
2. Prepare captions for a film-strip in about 18 frames on the Story of Job.
   or
   Draw a strip cartoon of some of the incidents in the story.
3. We often speak of the "patience of Job" and of "Job's comforters". How have these phrases arisen and what do they mean?
4. Find a record of "I know that my Redeemer liveth" from Handel's *Messiah*. Look up the words, then play the record. What do these words mean to us today? Part of the solo contains words from 1 Cor. xv, 20. What do these words mean?
5. Learn Job xxviii, 12–20, 23, 24, 26–28. Print "The fear . . . understanding" as large as you can for classroom display.
6. Prepare from the text of Job a play suitable for producing in Morning Assembly. It should have a prologue and an epilogue. There is an excellent guide in the Shorter Oxford Bible (O.U.P.), pp. 234–244.
7. Jonah sailed from Joppa to Tarshish. The boat was more than likely a Phoenician trading ship. Draw it. What cargo might it be carrying?
8. Could Jonah "run away from God"? Why did he think he could? What might he have thought of Psalm cxxxix, 1–12? What lesson did he learn?
9. What kind of a person is spoken of today as a "Jonah"? Why?
10. Dramatise the casting of lots that ended in Jonah's being thrown overboard.
11. As one of the court, report in your own words to the king the news of Jonah's preaching. What was the king's reply?
12. Read again the questions God asked of Jonah. What answers might Jonah have given after thinking about his experiences?

TIME CHART

OLD TESTAMENT   (*c.*=*circa*=about)

DATES B.C.	THE LAND AND THE PEOPLE	THEIR LEADERS AND RULERS		PEOPLE OF OTHER LANDS	EVENTS IN OTHER LANDS
c. 3000 –2350	Palestine a highway in the FERTILE CRESCENT for movements of people between Egypt and the Ancient East	NOMADIC leaders		ANCIENT CIVILISATIONS in the valleys of the Nile a Tigris-Euphrates	
c. 2100 –1700	Hebrews leave Ur for Palestine	*Patriarchs*	Abraham		Ancient Babylon now gre
c. 1700 –1600?	Hebrews in Egypt		Joseph	Hammurabi and Code of Laws	Tell-el-Amarna letters
c. 1350? 1300	The EXODUS Philistines settling in Palestine Hebrews enter Palestine		Moses		Hittites powerful
		Judges	Joshua, Deborah, Gideon, Samson	Philistines growing strong	Babylon weakening
1030	Tribes being united		Samuel		Assyrian power beginning
1010	War against Philistines	*Kings*	Saul		
			David		
970	1st temple built		Solomon		Phoenicia important